THE ULTIMATE
Low-Fat
MEXICAN
COOKBOOK

All the flavor without all the guilt

Gulf Publishing Company
Houston, Texas

THE ULTIMATE
Low-Fat
MEXICAN
COOKBOOK

All the flavor without all the guilt

Anne Lindsay Greer

The Ultimate Low-Fat Mexican Cookbook

Gulf Publishing Company
Book Division
P.O. Box 2608 □ Houston, Texas 77252-2608

10   9   8   7   6   5   4   3   2

Printed in Hong Kong

Library of Congress Cataloging-in-Publication Data

Greer, Anne Lindsay.
   The ultimate low-fat Mexican cookbook / Anne Lindsay Greer.
      p.   cm.
   Includes index.
   ISBN 0-87719-258-8 (acid-free paper)
   1. Cookery, Mexican. 2. Low-fat diet—Recipes. I. Title.
TX716.M4G743   1995
641.5′638—dc20   94-35995
                                                             CIP

Interior Book Design by Roxann L. Combs
Book Layout by Senta Eva Rivera
Photographs by Greg Milano

Cover photo shows three Salads: Tortilla Salad (center), Southwestern Bean Salad (in tamale husk), and Taco Salad (in tortilla shell) (Recipes on pages 78, 73, and 76)

To Jacqueline Earls and William McKenzie for their good-natured assistance, to Greg Milano for his endless patience and time, to Joyce Alff, my editor, and especially to Kelly.

CONTENTS

High in Flavor— Low in Fat

Whether you call it Tex-Mex, Mexican, or Southwestern food, the spirited flavors of tortilla specialties and mesquite grilled dishes create an insatiable desire in almost everyone for salsa, quesadillas, tacos, and enchiladas. Interestingly enough, the main ingredients in Mexican cooking—beans, corn, rice, tortillas, chilies, and tomatoes—are low in fat and high in nutritional value.

However, these ingredients have often been cooked in ways that are incompatible with a low-fat lifestyle. Historically, the introduction of animal fat did wonders for dishes using traditional Mexican or Indian ingredients, particularly in isolated regions where ingredients were sparse. Today, a new interest in health, fitness, and suitable low-fat foods makes some of the old ways obsolete. Reduced-fat products and recipes that use them innovatively make eating healthfully so much easier.

Save and Spend

The key to low-fat, flavorful eating is to "save and spend." By carefully counting calories and fat grams without sacrificing flavor, you can spend a few extra on a special dish. For example, what you save by softening tortillas for enchiladas in a nonstick skillet with vegetable cooking spray, you can spend on a Cookie Taco or a dollop of light sour cream.

The recipes in this book show you how to prepare traditional and contemporary Mexican and Southwest food with techniques that minimize unnecessary or excess fat. This is not a diet book nor is it a complicated technique book. The portions are realistic, the servings generous, and the recipes simple and straightforward. All the recipes have been tested and tasted by Mexican food *aficionados*, who in some cases, were surprised that the fat grams and calories were lower than they expected. The "save and spend" approach targets the high fat culprits in Mexican food so you can "spend" moderately.

Use the recipes and techniques as a guide and trust your personal taste as you begin cooking low fat. Remember, fat is like salt—it is easier to add than take away.

COOKING LIGHT

Lighter, low-fat cooking can be achieved in several ways. Use lean cuts of meat and remove all visible fat from fish and poultry either before or after cooking. Cooking without oil or using only a small amount of oil saves about 120 calories and 12 fat grams per tablespoon. Dramatic amounts of fat are saved by using a variety of cooking sprays.

Cooking sprays have many uses other than sautéing. Butter-flavored sprays are good for softening or baking tortillas. The olive oil sprays may be used on tossed salad greens, grilled vegetables, fish, or poultry. Many of the recipes for tacos, enchiladas, fajitas, and grilled fish emphasize seasoning, herbs, and chilies in place of fats and oils. Fresh fruits and vegetables are used generously in main dishes and accompaniments to add flavor instead of fat.

The Ultimate Low-Fat Mexican Cookbook contains recipes for a wide variety of salsas that give bright, spirited, "fat-free" flavor and color to foods. These salsas may be used with tortilla chips, on grilled fish, with quesadillas, or as a base for a light vinaigrette. You will find many recipes for beans—mashed, marinated, or in combinations—that are high in satisfaction, low in fat. There are Crab, Spinach, and Roasted Pepper Quesadillas that make light, bite-size hors d'oeuvres as well as a low-fat version of the popular layered party dip. Because cheese is relatively high in fat and calories, the recipes use low-fat cheese in smaller amounts than most recipes for tacos, enchiladas, and nachos. The texture and melting qualities are not as smooth as the regular cheeses, so you might choose to "spend" a few calories and fat grams here and use the "real thing." A bowl of chili (without the cheese) often has less fat and fewer calories than guacamole. Chicken Enchiladas with Tomatillo Sauce, Soft Chicken Tacos, or Grilled Chicken Tacos are quite good with half the amount of cheese most recipes call for. Cheese Enchiladas with Chili Sauce are made with a combination of cheeses and are significantly lighter than their restaurant versions. By using the recipe for Skinny Guacamole and reducing the cheese, a typical Taco Salad loses 15 to 20 fat grams and 200 to 300 calories.

LOW-FAT SUBSTITUTES

The Ultimate Low-Fat Mexican Cookbook emphasizes techniques that minimize unnecessary or excess fat. The section on tortillas presents simple techniques for "oven toasting" tortilla chips, tacos, and chalupa shells without the mess or calories from frying. You can make your own tostadas using a butter-flavored spray and a little salt that taste good and are sturdy enough to scoop up dips and salsas or support nacho toppings.

The Fat-Free or Smoked Turkey Stock gives delicious flavor to beans, soups, or enchilada sauces. You can enhance the flavors of dishes with low-fat herb and chile pestos, marinades, and basting sauces. Lean poultry and fish benefit from brief marinating to both season and tenderize. Very little fat is absorbed and surface fats are quickly burned off on a hot grill.

New products, such as fat-free cream cheese or low-fat ricotta cheese, give beans and sauces a creamy texture. Low-fat buttermilk and fat-free cream cheese combine to make a Sour Cream Sauce with a fraction of the fat grams and calories in sauces made from sour cream.

When using these recipes, always let your taste be your guide. If the sauce tastes good, there's no need for extra fat and calories from sour cream, whole milk, or mayonnaise-based dressings. But a low-fat meal is not destroyed if you use a little "real" sour cream here and there or indulge in a guacamole salad. Moderation is the key. "All or nothing" can take the fun out of food very quickly.

In all of the recipes, I've emphasized the ingredients that are naturally lean and have used low-fat substitutes wherever possible. Many recipes are enhanced by adding fresh vegetables. For example, Mexican Rice uses a variety of vegetables that contributes both color and flavor. Skinny Guacamole is made with green chilies, tomatillos, and non-fat sour cream and extends one avocado into four generous servings. An added benefit is that the citric acid from the tomatillos and green chilies helps preserve the bright green color. Egg whites and egg substitutes are used in place of whole eggs, and light mayonnaise takes the place of oil in cornbread. The idea that cornbread must have generous amounts of cream, butter, or bacon fat to be tender is somewhat outdated. Adding sautéed onions and using fat substitutes gives very satisfying results. The recipe for Cornmeal Crepes has less fat and fewer calories than corn tortillas and can be a delicious substitute for tortillas when making enchiladas. Salads are kept lean by preparing low-oil vinaigrettes and adding well-seasoned grilled meats and vegetables.

While the desserts in this book are not all low calorie, they are very low in fat. Fortunately, caramelized sugar doesn't have fat grams. My favorite dessert is the Cookie Taco, which is a crisp sugar shell filled with fresh berries and laced with both caramel and chocolate sauces with only 4 fat grams per taco. The "save and spend" philosophy allows for seconds!

CALORIES AND FAT GRAMS

All the recipes have been professionally analyzed for fat grams and calories. This led to some interesting discoveries. The same recipe analyzed by different organizations had slightly different fat grams and calories.

In this book, calories are rounded off to the nearest whole number and fat grams to the nearest decimal or half decimal point. If the garnish is part of the dish, it is included unless otherwise noted. In most recipes, fat grams and calories are per serving unless marked "per taco" or "per tablespoon."

All figures, however, should be treated as approximate. Knowing where the fat is, hidden or obvious, is helpful when planning menus for family and friends.

EATING LIGHT WHILE EATING OUT

Eating light when eating out is another challenge. Armed with some fat information and low-fat cooking techniques, it's easier to see where the fat is in Mexican food. While table salsa is "free," the chips are loaded with fat and calories, and it is easy to consume hundreds of calories before you order your dinner. I'm not suggesting you give up your weekly Mexican meal, but here are a few suggestions for lightening up.

- Order soft corn tortillas instead of (or in addition to) the complimentary basket of chips.
- Start with tortilla soup (without the cheese), ceviche, or a chicken taco instead of a platter of cheese-drenched nachos.
- Tell the waiter you want fajitas without any added fat.
- Order chicken enchiladas with red chile sauce or ranchero sauce with sour cream on the side.
- Use salsa on your taco salad.
- Omit all salad dressings and use salsa instead.

Mexican restaurants are second only in popularity to Italian. Even hard-core Tex-Mex eateries have lightened up and offer more choices, including grilled chicken, seafood items, and entrée salads. The fun, irresistible flavors and festive personality of Mexican food *can* fit into a fat-conscious lifestyle.

BASICS

Certain cooking techniques and recipes can dramatically reduce fats and oils while adding delicious flavors to foods. Try the tips and recipes that follow for preparing tortillas, chilies, soup stocks, and beans. Soon they will become basic procedures you will use again and again in countless recipes.

Food presentation and garnish is equally important, and the fun, whimsical nature of Mexican food, coupled with colorful natural ingredients, lends itself to creative garnishes that can almost always be low in fat.

Seasoning is very important in all cooking—it's what gives food "soul" and makes it memorable and satisfying. A pinch of cayenne gives cornmeal crepes personality. Cilantro and green chili pestos will brighten all your sauces and fillings. Smoky, spicy stocks liven up soups, chili, and enchilada sauces.

◀ *Fajita (front right), Shrimp and Scallop Ceviche (left front), Tostada Grande (back left), and Crab Quesadillas and Poblano Cream (back right)* (Recipes on pages 100, 54, 64, 56, and 37)

Oven-Fried Tortillas

Chalupas, chips and salsa, taco shells, and chiliquilas—they are all fried, resulting in fat and calories. The good news is that one corn tortilla is only about 50 calories with 1 gram of fat. The bad news is one small chip is about 30 calories with 1 to 2 grams of fat. One way to cut down on fat calories is to "oven toast" your own tortillas. The following instructions will tell you how to prepare basic chips and strips as well as decorative bowls and shells for salads and desserts.

Taco Shells

Spray corn tortillas on both sides with a butter-flavored spray. Drape upside down over two rungs on the middle oven rack. Bake at 350° for about 10 to 12 minutes or until crisp.

Tortillas will soften before getting crisp, so at first you may not think this will work. Be patient; it works.

Tortilla Chips

Cut tortillas into 6 or 8 pieces and spread out in a single layer on cookie sheets. Spray on both sides with a butter-flavored spray and sprinkle lightly with salt. Bake at 350° for 8 to 10 minutes or until crisp.

Tortilla Strips

Cut tortillas in thirds, then again in very thin strips. Spray the strips with a butter-flavored spray and sprinkle with salt. Bake on cookie sheets at 350° for 5 to 8 minutes or until crisp. Flour tortillas may be toasted in the same way.

Chalupa Shells

Spread tortillas in a single layer on a cookie sheet. Spray on both sides with a butter-flavored spray and sprinkle lightly with salt. Bake at 350° for 10 to 15 minutes or until crisp.

Tortilla Cups

Both corn and flour tortillas may be shaped into "taco bowls" or cups to hold salads, ice cream, fresh berries, or scrambled eggs. Many of the fillings, such as the Mushroom Filling (p. 52) or Chalupa toppings, are attractive served in tortilla cups.

Preheat oven to 350°. Spray the tortillas on both sides with a butter-flavored spray. To soften tortillas, place them directly on the oven rack for 1 minute. Remove and shape in one of the following ways:

- Press 5- to 6-inch diameter tortillas into muffin containers or 12-ounce Pyrex cups to make small bowls.
- Press burrito-sized tortillas in large ovenproof bowls to make salad shells for taco salads. Bake 12 to 15 minutes or until crisp. Flour tortillas should be lightly browned.

Corn Tortilla (1)
Fat grams 1
Calories 48

Flour Tortilla (1)
Fat grams 2
Calories 96

CHILIES: FACT, FOLKLORE, AND FUN

Chilies are named for their color (chile Colorado), their use (chile de ristra), their shape (chile ancho), their place of origin (chile Anaheim or Chimaya) or their hotness (Numero 6). No other ingredient resists standardization with such persistence or has enjoyed almost ritualistic attention. Although originally used to enhance an otherwise bland diet, chilies quickly became one of the first "health foods" and were used for medicinal purposes. They were once also used as currency, and as an aid to discourage thumb sucking in children. Chilies were thought to cure everything from a common cold to indifference towards romance. Current research suggests there could be more truth than folklore in such beliefs. Chilies may block cancer-causing compounds found in meats and may increase your metabolism, hastening weight loss. Some statements about chilies remain undisputed:

- Chilies have no fat and are high in vitamins A and C (higher than citrus).
- Chilies are low in calories.
- Chilies serve as a natural meat preservative by retarding the oxidation of fats.
- Chilies add personality and flavor to a variety of foods.
- Once included in your cooking, you might possibly become addicted.

This book limits chilies to a few varieties, all easily found in your supermarket. Many chili powders, dried chilies, and fresh chilies are also available in specialty markets. Most commercial brands, particularly generic chili powder and cayenne pepper, will be blends of various chilies. When cooking with chili pods, you will find it necessary to balance the earthy, sometimes bitter flavors with brown sugar, dried or fresh fruits, maple syrup, citrus, or vinegar. Tomatoes or tomatillos are often used to balance chili sauces and reduce the heat. Fats, such as bacon fat, cream, or butter, are a natural balance for chilies. That's why cheese, chili sauces, and copious amounts of sour cream are such tasty combinations. I've avoided these techniques in the recipes or limited their use to lower the fat and calories without sacrificing the delicious flavors that make these foods irresistible. I was surprised and delighted to find that a little cheese goes a long way, and many of the new low-fat or fat-free products are quite acceptable.

Dried Chilies

Chile Ancho: This is the dried poblano chili that has a distinctive wrinkled skin and flat wide shape. It is the chili used for chili con carne. It can be mild to hot with an earthy flavor.

Toast chilies before using in a 300° oven for about 8 minutes, then soak in water to rehydrate. Remove stems, seeds, and skin before using in soups, stews, or sauces.

Red Chili: The dried Anaheim or New Mexico chili has a smooth skin and long narrow shape. Rumored to be as unpredictable as a woman, it varies from very mild to incendiary with an addictive flavor. Prepare in the same way described above.

Chipotle: This chili is usually found canned, although its recent popularity has encouraged grocers to stock it in a dried state. Canned chipotles are packed in a smoky, very hot sauce. This is the dried jalapeño, which gives you a clue to its heat level. Use it sparingly and you'll love the flavors. This chili is a favorite among chefs for barbecue and meat sauces.

Fresh Chilies

Fresh chilies should be roasted and peeled to remove bitter, tough skins. Protect your hands with gloves or a generous coating of oil. "Capsaicin," the substance that makes chilies hot, resists soap and water and remains on your hands a long time, so don't rub your eyes after cutting or peeling chilies. If blending or disposing of seeds in a disposal, try not to inhale deeply or you might lose your voice temporarily. You can see where the saying, "It took a brave man to eat the first jalapeño, but a Texan to eat the second," might have come from. Don't let these cautionary instructions prevent you from working with fresh chilies. Your reward will be spirited flavors that give personality and soul to your cooking.

Green Chili: This is a smooth skinned, light green chili shaped like a small banana. Both its name and heat level are not easily recognized but, in general, New Mexico chilies are significantly hotter than Anaheim chilies. This is the chili used for canning. The skin is thinner than the poblano chili, making these chilies more difficult to work with when peeling or stuffing. They can be mild to hot.

Poblano Chili: This is a large, dark green chili shaped somewhat like a bell. Its thick skin and rich flavor make it ideal for stuffing or dicing and for adding flavor to soups, sauces, and quesadillas. Heat levels will vary with the season and growing area, but the poblano chili is usually moderately hot with a pleasant heat level. When dried, this becomes the chili ancho.

Jalapeño: This chili is small and dark green or red. It has a thick flesh and is hot to very hot. Jalapeños are often canned or sliced and pickled in glass jars. The heat is in the seeds and veins, so removing these allows you to enjoy the flavor with less bite. Jalapeños have a forward, lip-searing heat that can be tempered with milk, sour cream, or something sweet. Water is useless. There is a new, bright red jalapeño-shaped chili that is mild and makes a wonderful garnish.

Serrano: This is a very thin, light green chili that is as hot as the jalapeño. Although the heat is less "forward," it builds with each bite. It does not need to be roasted and peeled when used in relishes and salsas. However, you will want to remove the skin if it has been roasted. These chilies are hot to very hot.

Habanero: These are small bell-shaped chilies in bright green, red, and orange colors and are extremely hot. They may be used to make colorful accent creams and sauces (see the garnish section) or "conversational" table decorations.

To Roast and Peel Fresh Green Chilies

You may use your broiling element, electric range, gas burner, or outdoor grill.

Broiling: Preheat the broiler on the highest temperature. Place the chilies on a cookie sheet, directly under the broiler, and leave the door ajar. Roast until lightly charred and then turn to char all sides.

Range Top: Place a heat-proof rack atop your element and turn the heat to high. Place the chilies on the rack and roast until lightly charred. Turn the chilies to char all sides. They may jump a bit or sizzle and crackle—this is normal.

Gas Range: Spear chilies with a fork and place over the flame, turning to roast and char all sides.

Outdoor Grill: Roasting chilies over an outdoor charcoal grill will give the best flavor and aroma. Place them on the grill, close to the coals, and roast until lightly charred. Turn to char all sides. An indoor grill also works well; however, the charcoal flavors are absent.

In all cases, place the hot, charred chilies in a freezer bag and seal tightly. Let the chilies "steam" for 5 to 10 minutes and then remove stems, seeds, and peel. Chilies may be frozen, unpeeled, in freezer bags for a later use; however, the texture will not be as firm.

Roasting chilies indoors is a project that can set off your smoke alarm, so be forewarned but not dissuaded. The aromatic flavors of fresh roasted chilies are well worth the effort.

GARNISHES AND PRESENTATION

Restaurateurs and chefs spend as much time and energy in the presentation of their dishes as in their preparation. Contemporary Mexican or Southwestern dishes employ a variety of colorful, edible garnishes—quite a contrast to the typical monochromatic Tex-Mex plate of beans, enchiladas, and tamales. The availability of red and blue tortillas, a variety of lettuces, bell peppers, chilies, and tomatoes in brilliant shades of red, orange, and yellow, all contribute to the visual appeal of Mexican food. I suspect the popularity of black beans is in part due to the color contrast they provide on the plate.

A sprinkling of crumbled feta cheese, thinly sliced radishes, or a colorful salsa can transform an enchilada plate. Rice flecked with a variety of vegetables or chili-studded spoon bread served on a fringed tamale husk creates a plate with visual appeal. Spicy creams made from chilies or chili powder can be drizzled over mild sauces or soups. Tomatillo husks or bell peppers may be used as "ramekins" for salsas or side dishes. Dried or green corn husks can line a pie plate for a tamale pie or contain a sweet or savory corn pudding.

Most of the edible garnishes that follow have little or no fat and supply color, texture, and contrasting flavors to the Mexican dishes in this book. Make use of the wonderful array of chilies and natural ingredients to give your food a professional, appetizing appearance.

Crispy Greens

Thinly slice lettuces of contrasting colors—red tip leaf lettuce, Romaine, red cabbage, radicchio, spinach, or green leaf lettuce—and top with a sprinkling of toasted tortilla strips or pumpkin seeds and diced tomatoes. Use to garnish enchilada plates, combination plates, or entrées.

Spicy Creams

Roasted chilies or chili powders can be blended into colorful creams to garnish soups, salads, or tortilla specialties. They are quite hot, so use them on milder soups or sauces or to serve as a dipping sauce for quesadillas or tortilla chips. Purée the roasted, seeded chilies in a blender with 1 to 2 ounces fat-free cream cheese and use a little chicken broth to aid blending. Blend until very smooth, adding 1 to 2 tablespoons warm safflower oil as the blender runs. Season with salt, pepper, and a squeeze of lime juice. For green chilies, add generous sprigs of parsley to intensify the color. For red chilies, add a small amount of tomato paste.

If using cayenne pepper or chili powder, heat 1 to 2 tablespoons oil in a small skillet and add 2 tablespoons powder. Stir a few seconds, then transfer to a blender jar and blend with 1 tablespoon tomato paste and 2 to 3 tablespoons chicken broth. Use enough broth to make a consistency of heavy cream. Season to taste with salt and pepper. Dry chili pods may also be used to make accent creams. Simmer them in hot water until softened. Seed, stem, and peel the chilies. Purée in a blender with enough chicken broth to make a smooth thick sauce. Strain to remove skin if necessary. Add 1–2 tablespoons maple syrup to balance flavors. Season with salt and pepper.

Salsas

All of the fresh salsas make attractive garnishes for tortilla specialties, entrées, and soups. Choose complimentary colors and flavors. A simple combination of diced jicama, fresh corn, cilantro, and fresh lime juice is delicious with red or chili enchilada sauces. Fruits such as mango and papaya also go well with a variety of sauces, particularly sauces made with chilies or chili powder. Try a black bean salsa in place of beans. Use your imagination!

Edible Garnishes

Californians are fond of sour cream and black olives to garnish many Cal-Mex dishes. Low-fat Crema (p. 21) makes a good substitute and a neutral background for olives, green scallions, toasted tortilla strips, or thin strips of spinach or lettuces. There are a variety of low-fat cheeses on the market you can substitute for the traditional longhorn cheddar or Monterey Jack cheese.

The slightly tart, salty flavor of low-fat feta or goat cheese is delicious with many dishes, particularly those using tomatillos, wild mushrooms, chili sauces, or seafood. The new light processed American cheese makes it possible to make a significantly lighter Chili con Queso. Think of cheese as a garnish—you'll save fat and calories.

Corn Husks

Dried and green corn husks may be used to make "containers" for side dishes or to line a pie pan for tamale pie. Both need to first be soaked in hot water to soften them. Many enchilada casseroles are enhanced by attractive "fringed" corn husks around the edges.

To make individual corn husk containers, use a large husk. Clean and soak the husk until it is pliable. Tie a string or thin strip of husk around the narrow end, leaving about 3 inches above the tie. Fringe the ends and place in a flame to brown the edges. (They will not burn easily because they are wet). Turn the wide portion inside out. (This helps maintain the shape). To hold their shape, freeze the husk containers until ready to use.

Use the husks for salads, spoon bread, or sweet desserts such as rice pudding.

Chilies and Peppers

Jalapeño chilies, fresh and pickled, have been favorite garnishes for nachos. A new variety of jalapeño has been introduced that is red and mild. Slice them into "wheels" to garnish tostadas or nachos or use them whole to garnish appetizer trays. Small hot chilies are now available in many shapes and colors. These also make attractive garnishes, but warn your guests to nibble with caution. Roasted and peeled poblano chilies may be stuffed with side dishes as well as meats. Bell peppers make colorful containers for bean or corn salads or rice dishes.

Corn and flour tortillas may also be shaped and toasted in many shapes and sizes for garnish or to make bowls and containers. See the section on Oven-Fried Tortillas for more ideas and techniques.

In some areas corn tortillas are available in blue and red as well as white or yellow. Thinly sliced and baked, they make festive, crunchy garnishes for salads, soups, or entrée plates.

Use fresh herbs such as parsley, generous sprigs of basil, oregano, and cilantro. Italian parsley is particularly sturdy and less prone to rapid wilting. After rinsing fresh herbs, dry thoroughly and store them in paper towel-lined zip-lock bags to keep them fresh and crisp.

Citrus "wheels" make a colorful, attractive garnish for entrée or combination plates. To make these, thinly slice seedless oranges or limes and make one cut half-way through the center of each slice. Grasp the cut ends and twist one-quarter turn to make a spiral shape. A combination of an orange slice, beet slice, and parsley sprig is often used in restaurants to garnish a plate.

Mexican food has many colorful natural ingredients to make garnishing innovative and fun. Make generous use of fresh herbs, edible flowers, colorful chilies, and refreshing salsas to enhance your hard work!

CHICKEN PREPARATION

To Grill Chicken

To grill chicken to use in salads, soups, or quesadillas, use boneless, skinned chicken breasts. Marinate the chicken breasts for 3 to 4 hours in the following marinade:

Marinade:

1 1/2	cups safflower oil
1/2	cup vinegar
3	tablespoons soy sauce
2	jalapeño chilies, chopped
5	cloves garlic, minced
	Juice from 2 lemons
1/2	cup chicken broth
1/2	tablespoon coarsely ground black pepper
1/2	tablespoon sea salt

Preheat the grill to the highest setting. Remove chicken from the marinade and grill over high heat until well marked, about 4 minutes. Turn to cook the other side, brushing with marinade at least once. Cook 3 to 4 minutes and remove. If preparing chicken in advance to be used cold in salads or to be added to soup or quesadillas, seal the cooked chicken tightly in plastic wrap and refrigerate until ready to use. After slicing, season the chicken again with salt and pepper.

Fat grams and calories: The amount of oil absorbed in marinating chicken is minimal—less than one tablespoon per chicken breast.

To Cook Chicken and Prepare for Tacos, Enchiladas, Fillings

The chicken will retain more moisture and flavor if cooked on the bone. First trim away large pieces of fat but leave the skin intact. Preheat the oven to 400°. Season the chicken pieces with salt and pepper and roast for 30 to 35 minutes. When cool enough to handle, remove skin, bones, and any remaining fat. Use two forks to shred the meat, or cut into bite-sized pieces. Season with salt and coarsely ground black pepper.

Seasoned Chicken Filling

5	chicken breasts, on the bone
	Salt and pepper
1	onion, chopped
1	green bell pepper, chopped
1	cup canned tomatoes, juices drained, chopped
1/2	teaspoon garlic salt
	Salt and pepper to taste

Optional:

2	jalapeño chilies, stemmed, seeded, diced

Preheat the oven to 400°.

Season chicken with salt and pepper and place in roasting pan. Roast for 30 to 35 minutes. When cool enough to handle, use two forks to shred the meat, discarding all fat, bones, and skin. Set aside.

Heat a medium skillet over medium heat. Spray generously with a vegetable coating spray. Add the onion and bell pepper and sauté, stirring a few times to prevent burning. (You may need to add additional spray). When the onions are soft and lightly browned, add the chopped tomatoes and season to taste. Stir the tomato-onion mixture into the chicken and toss well.

For a spicier filling, stir in the jalapeño chilies.

Fills
10 tacos or
enchiladas

Fat grams
2 per 1/3 cup

Calories
90 per 1/3 cup

FAT-FREE STOCK

*Makes about
2 1/2 cups*

*Fat grams
3–4*

*Calories
40 per cup*

This flavorful, rich stock has very little fat and is packed with flavor. It takes much less time than you might think and cooks with very little supervision. Use it when cooking beans or as a substitute for chicken broth in enchilada sauces. You may double or triple the recipe if you have a large stock pot.

2	pounds salt pork, fat trimmed
3	smoked ham hocks, fat trimmed
3–6	chicken wings, optional
2	large onions, coarsely chopped
6	cloves garlic, coarsely chopped
1	large stalk celery, in pieces
1	large carrot, in pieces
10	parsley sprigs
6–7	cups water
1	14 1/2-ounce can chicken or beef broth

Trim excess fat from ham hocks and salt pork. Don't worry about leaving some of the fat. You will skim it off later.

Preheat the oven to broil. Spray the vegetables and garlic with a little vegetable coating spray and place vegetables and chicken wings in a roasting pan on the middle rack. Cook about 8 to 10 minutes, turning several times to brown. Transfer to a large saucepan and add the ham hocks and salt pork. Fill the saucepan with water and chicken broth. Add parsley and bring to a boil. Skim the foam from the top and reduce to a simmer.

Simmer the stock at least 1 1/2 hours or up to 3 hours. Add more water if cooking the maximum time. The longer you cook the stock, the more intense the flavors.

Cool the vegetables in the stock, then strain and discard the bones and vegetables. Refrigerate the stock until the fat solidifies and is easy to remove.

Store in 1 cup containers or zip-lock bags.

Smoked Turkey Stock

....

The method for making this stock is similar to that for Fat-Free Stock. The sweetness of the smoked chicken or turkey makes the finished stock particularly good for preparing enchilada sauces made from dried chili pods. I usually make stock in large quantities when I have a smoked turkey and freeze it in 1-cup freezer bags.

*Makes about
2 1/2 to 3 cups*

*Fat grams
3–4 per cup*

*Calories
50 per cup*

	Meaty bones from a smoked turkey or
	2 smoked chickens
	Water to cover
2	large onions, coarsely chopped
6	cloves garlic, chopped
2	large stalks celery, coarsely chopped
12	parsley sprigs
2	sprigs fresh thyme
1	tablespoon cracked black pepper
	Water

Cut a large turkey carcass into smaller pieces to easily fit a large stock pot. Put all the ingredients in the stock pot and fill it with enough water to cover all the bones. Bring to a boil over high heat, skimming the foam from the top.

Reduce the heat to a simmer and simmer, uncovered, for 2 1/2 to 3 hours. (You may need to add additional water.)

Strain the stock and discard all bones and vegetables. Cool and refrigerate. Remove solidified fat from the stock and discard. Strain the stock again and store in 1 to 2 cup amounts in freezer bags. Add salt when using the stock for cooking. The stock may be frozen for 9 to 12 months.

Note: Browning the bones under the broiling element of your oven or on an outdoor grill will greatly enhance the flavor of the finished stock. Simply brown on both sides for 6 to 8 minutes.

CORNMEAL CREPES

....

Makes
25–28

Fat grams
1

Calories
45

Crepes made with cornmeal and seasoned with fresh herbs and chilies make a wonderful substitute for corn or flour tortillas. They are easier to roll, and you avoid the "oil drenched" method of preparing corn tortillas for enchiladas. When baked with enchilada fillings and sauces, they taste similar to tamales. Crepes do not dry out or get hard like tortillas, have fewer calories, and taste delicious. You may prefer these to corn tortillas. Stacked enchiladas and enchilada casseroles are particularly good when made with cornmeal crepes.

1/2	teaspoon cayenne pepper or
	2 serrano chilies, stemmed, seeded
2	sprigs fresh cilantro or parsley
	Egg substitute equivalent to 4 eggs
1	cup water
1	cup skim milk
1	teaspoon salt
1/2	teaspoon baking powder
1	cup cornmeal
1	cup all-purpose flour
1	tablespoon sugar
1 1/2	tablespoons safflower oil

Thoroughly mince the chilies and cilantro in a blender or food processor fitted with the metal blade. Add the egg substitute, water, milk, salt, baking powder, cornmeal, flour, sugar, and oil and blend until very smooth. Let the batter rest at room temperature 30 minutes to an hour.

Heat a well-seasoned crepe pan or small skillet over medium heat. Coat with a vegetable coating spray. When the pan is hot, add about 1/4 cup crepe batter. Tilt the pan, rotating so the batter is evenly distributed. Cook until the crepe appears dry, then turn and cook on the opposite side. Remove. Spray the pan again and repeat until all the batter has been used.

Store crepes between sheets of wax paper or plastic wrap until ready to use.

Advance Preparation: Crepes may be prepared a day in advance. They freeze quite well for 3 to 4 months.

BLACK BEANS

This seems like a lot of vegetables for 1 pound of beans, but they help give the stock good flavor and, if diced quite small, they tend to disappear. If you like the beans very soft or you plan to purée them for soup or a dip, increase the cooking time about 30 minutes.

*Makes about
6 cups*

*Fat grams
3 per cup*

*Calories
294 per cup*

1	pound black beans
1	large onion, finely diced
1	large carrot, finely diced
1	celery stalk, finely minced
1	jalapeño chili, stemmed and minced
3	cloves garlic, minced
2	14 1/2-ounce cans chicken broth or Fat-Free Stock (p. 14)
3/4	cup tomato sauce
3	cups water
3	large chunks smoked pork, all fat trimmed
1–2	teaspoons salt, or to taste

Garnish:

    Pico de Gallo (p. 24)
    Light sour cream

Soak the beans in enough water to cover for 3 to 4 hours or overnight. Drain and discard the water.

Preheat the oven to 500°. Coat the vegetables with a vegetable spray and place on the center rack. Roast the vegetables about 20 minutes, then turn the setting to "broil" and broil, turning several times, until lightly browned. Remove and cool. Cut into a fine dice. (This extra step vastly improves the flavor of the finished product.)

Coat a large saucepan with a vegetable spray and place over medium heat. Add the garlic and sauté, stirring constantly, to release flavor. Add the vegetables and cook until softened, about 5 minutes.

Add the broth, tomato sauce, water, and beans and bring to a boil. Skim foam from the top, reduce the heat to a simmer, and cook about 1 hour, stirring occasionally. Add salt after the beans are fully cooked. Remove smoked pork and discard. If you want a thicker broth, simply purée about 1 cup of the beans in a blender or food processor and mix them into the beans.

Serve beans with any of the tortilla specialties. Garnish with light sour cream and Pico de Gallo.

Pinto Beans: Cook pinto beans in the same manner. They will take about 30 minutes more time to cook and will require additional water.

QUICK BLACK BEANS

··

Makes
6 servings

Fat grams
2

Calories
250

There are many very acceptable bean products on supermarket shelves—a boon to the increasing number of working cooks! Use the same ingredients and method for pinto beans. This is a good place to use Smoked Turkey Stock or Fat-Free Stock.

2	14 1/2-ounce cans black beans, drained
2	cloves garlic, minced
1	cup diced onion
2	tablespoons finely minced bell pepper
1	1/2 ounce low-fat smoked sausage, minced
1	cup chicken or beef broth
1/4	cup tomato sauce
2	serrano chilies, stemmed, seeded, and minced
	Salt and pepper to taste

Drain the black beans, reserving all the juices.

Coat a medium saucepan with a vegetable spray and place over medium heat. Add the garlic and onion and sauté until softened. (You may need to use some additional vegetable spray.) Add the bell pepper and reserved juices from the beans. Simmer about 3 to 4 minutes, then add sausage, chicken broth, and tomato sauce and cook about 10 to 15 minutes. Stir in chilies and beans and cook just long enough to heat thoroughly to make a moderately thick broth. Season to taste with salt and pepper.

Advance Preparation: Beans may be prepared a day in advance.

MASHED BEANS

1	cup chopped onion
1/2	teaspoon chili powder
1–2	teaspoons chicken broth or water
1/2	cup low-fat ricotta cheese
1/2	cup picante sauce
1/2	teaspoon garlic salt
2	cups cooked pinto or black beans (p. 17)
	Salt and pepper to taste

Makes
4 servings

Fat grams
2

Calories
200

Coat a medium skillet generously with a vegetable spray and cook the onion over medium heat, stirring constantly, until lightly browned. Stir in chili powder and 1 to 2 tablespoons chicken broth or water. Remove from heat and transfer to a food processor fitted with the metal blade.

Add the ricotta cheese, picante sauce, garlic salt, and beans. Process to purée. Season to taste with salt and pepper.

If serving beans as a side dish, bring beans to a simmer in a well-seasoned skillet over medium heat and cook until hot and thickened. Serve garnished with grated cheese, Crema (p. 21), or shredded iceberg lettuce and diced tomatoes.

If using for nachos, spread on toasted tortillas and top with cheese or desired toppings.

CILANTRO PESTO

Makes
1 cup

Fat grams
4 per tablespoon

Calories
40 per tablespoon

Use this to baste grilled fish, chicken, or meats, to season soups, rice, and dips, or wherever you want assertive seasoning.

4	cloves garlic, peeled
2	cups fresh parsley, stemmed (packed)
2	cups fresh cilantro, stemmed (packed)
4	tablespoons safflower oil
2	tablespoons pine nuts or almonds, toasted
1	tablespoon Parmesan cheese
1	teaspoon lemon juice
1/4	teaspoon salt
	Pinch white pepper

In a blender or food processor, combine all the ingredients until well mixed. Store in a covered container.

If using as a basting sauce, add 1 cup chicken or beef broth and 1/2 cup oil.

SPICY GREEN CHILI PESTO

Makes
1 1/4 cups

Fat grams
3 per tablespoon

Calories
33 per tablespoon

You can use this to season rice, top broiled fish, or add to dips when you want to add flavor and spice.

5	serrano chilies, stemmed, seeded or
	1 large poblano chili, roasted, peeled, seeded
2	cups fresh parsley, stemmed (packed)
2	cups fresh cilantro, stemmed (packed)
5	cloves garlic
2	tablespoons pumpkin seeds or pine nuts, toasted
1	tablespoon Parmesan or Romano cheese, grated
4	tablespoons safflower oil
	Squeeze of fresh lime juice
1/4–1/2	teaspoon salt

Using a blender or a food processor fitted with the metal blade, process chilies, parsley, cilantro, garlic, and nuts. Blend until very finely chopped and combined. Add oil, lime juice, and salt to taste.

Store refrigerated for 2 days or freeze for about 2 months. While the flavors freeze well, the texture becomes somewhat soggy when frozen.

PUMPKIN SEED PESTO

Use this pesto to add to dips or stir into sour cream or Crema (recipe follows) to serve with tostadas.

*Makes
3/4 cup*

*Fat grams
4 per tablespoon*

*Calories
62 per tablespoon*

    4 cloves garlic
    3 cups Italian parsley, packed
    1/3 cup toasted pumpkin seeds
    3 tablespoons safflower oil
    pinch crushed red pepper (or to taste)
    salt to taste

Using a blender or food processor fitted with the metal blade, process the garlic, parsley, pumpkin seeds, oil, and red pepper flakes until finely chopped. Season to taste with salt.

CREMA

Use this in place of sour cream and save significant fat grams and calories. If you prefer a richer taste, substitute light sour cream for the nonfat sour cream, and you'll still trim the fat.

*Makes
2 cups*

*Fat grams
trace*

*Calories
8 per tablespoon*

    1   cup nonfat or light sour cream
    1   cup plain, low-fat yogurt
    1/4   cup skim milk
             Pinch of salt and pepper

Using a whisk, whip the sour cream, yogurt, and skim milk until smooth.
Season to taste with salt and pepper.

SALSAS AND DIP

Seeing is deceiving. It's eating that's believing.

James Thurber

Simple table salsas, often called the "salt and pepper" of Mexican food, are equal to catsup in national popularity and retail sales. There are several varieties of picante sauces, some made with fresh tomatoes, others with good quality canned tomatoes. Flavors are perked up by grilling, roasting, or smoking the tomatoes, and, of course, by adding spicy little chilies. Some salsas are made with a wide variety of fruits, vegetables, and combinations of tomatillos, fruits, corn, and beans. These are almost *little salads*, and make a refreshing contrast to the robust flavors of Mexican dishes. They also add a colorful, nonfat garnish to enchilada plates or quesadillas. Variations are limited only by your imagination and personal taste.

You'll also find several appetizer dips and a Skinny Guacamole recipe in this section. The Chili Poblano Cream will satisfy chili *aficionados*, and you'll never miss the fat in the Bean Dip.

◄ *Four Salsas: Three Tomato Salsa (upper left), Jicama Salsa (lower left), Poblano Cream (upper right), Pico de Gallo (lower right)* (Recipes on pages 34, 35, 37, and 24)

Pico de Gallo

About
4 cups

Makes
8 servings

Fat grams
trace

Calories
35

You can adjust the amount and type of heat in this fresh salsa by the kind and amount of chili used. Serrano chilies produce a somewhat subtle "late" heat, while jalapeños give that forward "lip-searing" heat. Removing both seeds and membrane lessens the heat. This is a good basic salsa from which you can make many variations. I prefer using Roma tomatoes as they are usually better quality.

6	Roma tomatoes or
	3 ripe tomatoes
1	cup diced yellow or white onion or
	1–2 bunches scallions, sliced
3–4	serrano chilies, stemmed, seeded, diced fine or
	1–3 jalapeño chilies, stemmed, seeded,
	diced fine
	Juice from 1 lime
	Salt and white pepper to taste
1	tablespoon fresh cilantro, minced

Remove cores from tomatoes and cut evenly into 1/4-inch dice. Place in a glass bowl.

In a strainer, rinse onions under ice cold water to remove bitter liquids. Add to the tomatoes along with chilies and lime juice. Season to taste with salt, pepper, and cilantro.

Refrigerate 2 hours before using.

Avocado Salsa: Add 1 avocado peeled, cored, and diced, with additional lime juice, salt, and cilantro.

California Salsa: Add 1/2 cup each diced black and green olives and 1/2 cup toasted pumpkin seeds. Use scallions in place of white or yellow onions.

Black Bean Salsa: Add 1 cup well-seasoned, cooked black beans and 3/4 cups mango or papaya. Adjust seasonings by adding more lime juice and salt.

GRILLED CORN AND PEPPER SALSA

....

4	ears fresh corn, shucked
	Chili powder
	Salt and pepper
1	cup diced red onion
1–2	teaspoons safflower oil
1	green bell pepper, stemmed, seeded, diced
1	red bell pepper, stemmed, seeded, diced
2	serrano chilies, diced
	Fresh lime juice
	Salt and pepper to taste

Makes
3 1/2 cups
6 servings

Fat grams
2

Calories
71

Preheat an indoor or outdoor grill to the highest setting (or use the broiling element of your oven).

Generously coat the corn with a vegetable spray and sprinkle lightly with chili powder, salt, and pepper. Grill or broil on both sides 4 to 5 minutes. Using a sharp knife, cut corn kernels from the cob. Set aside.

Generously coat a medium skillet with vegetable spray and place over medium heat. Add the onion and sauté 1 to 2 minutes. Do not brown.

Combine onion, corn, bell peppers, and serrano chilies in a small bowl. Season with lime juice, salt, and pepper.

GRILLED TOMATO SALSA

Makes
8 servings

Fat grams
trace

Calories
17

This is my favorite table salsa that I learned to make from my good friend Jesse Calvillo. Smoking the tomatoes prior to grilling greatly enhances their flavor. This is the table salsa served at Jesse's restaurant, La Fogata, in San Antonio.

	Safflower oil
4–5	large, vine ripe tomatoes, cores intact
2–3	serrano chilies, stemmed
2	tablespoons fresh cilantro
	Salt and white pepper to taste
	Lime juice to taste

Preheat the oven to 300°.

Rub tomatoes with oil and place on an outdoor grill over high heat. Cover the grill and cook the tomatoes until they are lightly charred and the juices begin to flow, about 10 to 12 minutes. Turn tomatoes to expose all sides.

Remove tomatoes. Cut in half and place on an oiled cookie sheet. Roast in the oven 15 to 20 minutes or until very soft.

Put tomatoes and their juices in a blender with serrano chilies and blend smooth. (You will have to do this in several batches.) Season with cilantro, salt, pepper, and lime juice.

Note: If the salsa congeals, add 1 to 2 tablespoons vinegar and simmer over medium-low heat for 5–8 minutes. When tomatoes are not ripe, the salsa will not have a rich, red color. In this case, add 1 cup canned puréed tomatoes including juices.

QUICK TOMATO SALSA

This quick salsa is a good choice in winter months when ripe tomatoes are scarce.

1	clove garlic, minced
1	medium yellow onion, diced
1	4 1/2-ounce can green chilies
1	16-ounce can tomatoes
2–4	fresh jalapeño chilies, seeded, stemmed, diced
1	tablespoon red wine vinegar
	Salt and pepper to taste
1	tablespoon fresh cilantro, minced

Coat a medium skillet with a nonstick vegetable spray and place over medium heat. Add garlic and onion and sauté a few seconds. The idea is to cook the onions and garlic enough to release their flavor but keep them slightly crisp.

Add the green chilies to the onion mixture. Remove from the heat.

Using a blender or a food processor fitted with the metal blade, blend the tomatoes to purée. Combine tomatoes, chilies, jalapeños, and vinegar in a mixing bowl. Season to taste with salt, pepper, and cilantro. Store refrigerated.

Makes
8 servings

Fat grams
trace

Calories
35

CHUNKY SALSA

....

Makes
4 cups

Fat grams
2 per 1/2 cup

Calories
72 per 1/2 cup

1	16 1/2-ounce can Mexican-style stewed toma-
toes	
4	serrano or jalapeño chilies, stemmed, seeded
1 1/2	cups chopped onion
1	cup fresh tomatoes, diced, juices drained
1/2	cup tomato sauce
	Salt and pepper to taste
1	tablespoon fresh cilantro

Using a blender or food processor fitted with the metal blade, process serrano chilies and canned tomatoes to purée. Place in a non-reactive or glass bowl.

Coat a medium skillet with a vegetable spray and place over medium heat. Add onion and sauté 1 to 2 minutes, stirring constantly, until lightly browned. Add onion, fresh tomato, and tomato sauce to blended tomatoes and chilies. Season to taste with salt, pepper, and cilantro.

Chunky Ancho-Tomato Salsa

Soak 2 ancho chili pods in boiling chicken broth or water until soft. Stem, seed, and peel.

Using a blender, process the chilies with 2 tomatillos and 3–4 tablespoons chicken broth until smooth.

Stir into the prepared Chunky Tomato Salsa. Season to taste with salt and a pinch of sugar. Serve warm or at room temperature.

GREEN CHILI SALSA

This salsa is best when made with New Mexico green chilies. They are hotter than California Anaheim chilies and truly "set your heart and soul on fire." Try serving 3 or 4 salsas with toasted tortillas the next time you entertain guests. You'll find it fun to "mix and match." Serve this salsa warm or at room temperature.

Makes
2 1/2–3 cups
8 servings

Fat grams
3.5

Calories
80

1/2	pound ground round
2	cloves garlic, minced
1	onion, chopped
1–1 1/2	teaspoons salt
	Pinch white pepper
15–16	fresh green chilies (about 1 pound), roasted and peeled or 4 4 1/2-ounce cans diced green chilies
2	teaspoons to 1 tablespoon cider vinegar
	Pinch sugar (if needed)

Heat a medium skillet over medium-high heat. Put the meat in the hot pan and sear, without stirring, until browned, and juices no longer run red. When browned, break up the meat with a fork and add garlic and onion. Sauté until meat is fully cooked and onions are translucent. Season with salt and pepper.

Seed, stem, and dice fresh chilies about 1/4 inch in size. Add to the beef and onion mixture. Balance the flavors by adding vinegar and a pinch of sugar. Taste and adjust seasonings.

Serve with toasted tortilla chips.

TOMATILLO SALSA

Makes
6 servings

Fat grams
trace

Calories
20 per serving

Tomatillos have a slightly tart, citrus flavor. This is a very refreshing salsa that is particularly good with chicken or grilled salmon. Tomatillos, like lemons, vary in acidity. Adding some fruit helps balance any bitterness.

1/2	cup packed cilantro leaves
14	tomatillos, husks removed, rinsed, and quartered
2	serrano chilies, stemmed, seeded
2–3	pieces of ripe mango, papaya, or cantaloupe, about 1-inch square
1	clove garlic, minced
2	shallots, minced
2	tablespoons white wine
2	teaspoons fresh lime juice
	Salt to taste
	Pinch white pepper

Using a blender or food processor fitted with the metal blade, process the cilantro, tomatillos, chilies, and fruit until well blended. If using a blender, use on/off turns to prevent liquefying. You may need to do this in several batches.

Put the garlic and shallot in a small saucepan with the white wine and bring to a boil over medium heat to "sweat." Cool and blend with the tomatillos.

Season to taste with lime juice, salt, and white pepper. Refrigerate until ready to use.

MANGO SALSA

This is a refreshing summer salsa that is good with grilled chicken or fish and as a garnish for soft tacos. I particularly like it with Chicken Margarita. If you cannot find good mangoes, substitute ripe papayas.

Makes
6 servings

Fat grams
trace

Calories
46

1 1/2	cups diced mango
1	cup red onion, diced
2	tablespoons rice wine vinegar
	Ice water
1	cup diced red bell pepper, roasted and peeled
2	serrano chilies, stemmed, seeded, diced
1–2	teaspoons fresh lime juice
	Salt to taste
1	tablespoon fresh cilantro

Use firm, but ripe mango. Over-ripe fruits are difficult to dice because they turn to mush.

Put the onion in a shallow dish and cover with vinegar and ice water. Soak for 30 minutes. Strain.

In a glass bowl, gently combine the mango, onions, peppers, and chilies. Season to taste with lime juice, salt, and cilantro. Refrigerate for 1 hour before serving.

Pineapple-Pepper Salsa

*Makes
6 servings*

*Fat grams
trace*

*Calories
50*

Chilies marry well with fruits; they actually intensify the fruit flavor. This is very mild and goes well with pork, poultry, or breakfast tacos.

1/2	fresh pineapple, diced
1	small papaya, peeled, seeded, and diced
2–3	serrano chilies, seeded, stemmed, and diced
1	cup red onion, diced fine
1/2	cup red bell pepper, diced fine
	Juice from 1 lime
	Salt and white pepper to taste
1	teaspoon fresh basil or mint

Dice the pineapple and papaya in 1/8- to 1/4-inch sized dice.

Mix pineapple and papaya with serrano chilies in a glass bowl.

Coat a small skillet with vegetable spray and place on medium heat. Add the onion and cook until softened, about 1 minute.

Add the onion and bell pepper to the pineapple. Season with lime, salt, pepper, and herb of choice. Refrigerate 1 to 2 hours before using.

Grilled Red Snapper with Warm Shrimp Salsa, Black Beans, and Crispy Greens (Recipes on pages 106, 17, and 8)▶

Summer Melon Salsa

This is a colorful, slightly spicy salsa that is excellent with grilled fish or poultry. Choose melons that are ripe but firm and dice them in even, one-quarter-inch squares.

1	cup diced cucumber
1	cup diced cantaloupe melon
1	cup diced honeydew melon
1/2	cup diced red bell pepper
2	serrano chilies, seeded, stemmed, and minced
1	tablespoon rice wine vinegar
1	tablespoon minced basil or cilantro
	Salt and white pepper to taste

Combine all the ingredients in a glass bowl and season to taste with salt and pepper. Refrigerate 1 to 2 hours before serving.

*Makes
8 servings*

*Fat grams
trace*

*Calories
28*

THREE TOMATO SALSA

Makes
6 servings

Fat grams
trace

Calories
73

This is a colorful Pico de Gallo-type salsa that is very mild. Use it with grilled fish, on salads, or with fajitas and quesadillas.

1/4	cup white wine vinegar
1/2	cup red onion, diced
	Ice water
8	tomatillos, husks removed, rinsed, and diced 1/4 inch
1	pint yellow cherry tomatoes, diced 1/4 inch
4	Roma tomatoes, diced 1/4 inch
1–2	serrano chilies, stemmed, seeded, and minced
1–2	teaspoons fresh lime juice
	Salt to taste
1	tablespoon minced fresh basil or cilantro

Soak the onion in vinegar and ice water to cover for 30 minutes. Drain and toss with tomatillos, tomatoes, and serrano chilies.

Season to taste with fresh lime juice, salt, and basil or cilantro. Refrigerate at least 1 hour before using.

Jicama Salsa

When these ingredients are diced, the result is a pico de gallo-type salsa. If cut in julienne strips, they make an attractive little salad that can be used to garnish tortilla specialties.

*Makes
6 servings*

*Fat grams
trace*

*Calories
36*

1/2	small jicama, peeled
1	red bell pepper
1	yellow bell pepper
1	green bell pepper
1	carrot, peeled
	Juice from 1/2 lime
1	tablespoon rice wine vinegar
	Salt and pepper to taste
	Minced fresh cilantro

Thinly slice jicama and then cut into a 1/4-inch dice. Core and seed peppers and cut into 1/4-inch dice.

Blanch the carrot until you can pierce it with a fork, then rinse under cool water and dice 1/2 inch.

Combine all ingredients and toss with lime, vinegar, salt, pepper, and cilantro. Refrigerate several hours before using.

Jicama-Corn Relish

Omit the yellow bell pepper and carrot and add 1 cup fresh, cooked corn kernels. This simple relish goes well with spicy enchilada sauces.

SPICY BEAN DIP

Makes
3 cups

Fat grams
.5 per tablespoon

Calories
12 per tablespoon

2	cups cooked pinto or black beans
1/2	cup Quick Tomato Salsa (p. 27) or picante sauce
1/2	cup low-fat ricotta cheese
	Squeeze of lime juice
1	cup onion, chopped
3	jalapeño chilies, stemmed, seeded, diced
3–4	tablespoons chicken broth
1	teaspoon chili powder
1/2	teaspoon garlic salt
2	slices nonfat processed cheese, in pieces

Garnishes:

1/4	cup Poblano Cream (p. 37) or Crema (p. 21)
1/2	cup diced tomatoes or Pico de Gallo (p. 24)

Put the beans in a blender or food processor fitted with the metal blade and process smooth. Add salsa or picante sauce, ricotta cheese, and lime juice and blend.

Place a medium skillet over medium heat and coat with a vegetable spray. Add the onion and jalapeño chilies and cook 1 to 2 minutes or until lightly browned. Add the chicken broth, chili powder, and garlic salt. Simmer 3 to 4 minutes or until the liquid is reduced by about half. Add the processed cheese, stirring to melt.

Add the cooled onion mixture to the blended beans and process until smooth. Taste and adjust salt and pepper.

Serve the dip in a bowl garnished with a "drizzle" of Poblano Crema or Crema and diced tomatoes.

CHILI POBLANO CREAM

....

This spicy cream may be used as a dip or drizzled on beans, chalupas, soups, or tacos for a little spice.

1	tomatillo, skinned, rinsed, and quartered
6–8	sprigs parsley or cilantro
3	poblano chilies, roasted, peeled, seeded
3	ounces nonfat or light cream cheese
2–3	tablespoons chicken broth (if needed)
2	tablespoons warm safflower oil
	Fresh lime juice to taste
1/2	teaspoon garlic salt
	Salt to taste

*Makes
1 1/2 cups*

*Fat grams
2 per tablespoon*

*Calories
21 per tablespoon*

Using a blender, blend the tomatillos with parsley and chilies until smooth.

Add cream cheese in several pieces and blend smooth. You may need to add chicken broth to aid blending.

Heat the safflower oil and add it with the blender running to help emulsify the mixture. Season with lime juice and garlic salt. Add additional salt, if desired.

Store refrigerated until ready to use. The cream keeps well for 3 to 4 days. Reblend before using, if necessary.

QUESO

Makes
1 1/2 cups

Fat grams
2 per tablespoon

Calories
23 per tablespoon

Everything about "queso" is fat and calories. This version uses nonfat cream cheese and the new light processed cheese product, which cut both fat and calories by almost half. Every little bit counts!

1/2	onion, chopped
2/3	cup water
1/4	cup diced green bell peppers
1/4	cup diced red bell peppers
2	jalapeño chilies, minced or
	1/4 cup diced green chilies
5	ounces "light" or nonfat processed American
	cheese, in cubes
3	ounces nonfat cream cheese, in cubes
1/3	cup diced tomatoes

Heat a medium skillet over medium heat. Add onion and water and simmer 2 to 3 minutes. Add bell peppers, chilies, processed cheese, and cream cheese, stirring until cheese is smooth and melted.

Drain any juices from the tomatoes and mix into the queso. Serve with toasted tortilla chips or a variety of raw vegetables such as celery, carrots, or cauliflower. Queso will harden when it cools, but is easily melted again in a microwave oven.

SKINNY
GUACAMOLE

This is a chunky-style guacamole that extends one avocado and helps reduce fat and calories. For best results, buy avocados 2 or 3 days before using and let them ripen away from direct sunlight. Light sour cream, nonfat sour cream, and fat-free cream cheese all work well in this recipe. If you don't mind a few extra calories, use two avocados and add a little fresh lemon juice. The tomatillos help keep the color fresh.

Makes
4 servings

Fat grams
8

Calories
122

2	small tomatillos, skinned, rinsed, and quartered
1	clove garlic
1/4	cup diced green chilies
3	sprigs cilantro or parsley
1	avocado, peeled, pitted, and cut in several pieces
3	tablespoons light or nonfat sour cream
	Salt and pepper to taste
	Fresh lemon juice, optional
1/4	cup diced onion or scallion
1/3	cup diced fresh tomato

Using a blender or food processor, process the tomatillos with garlic, chilies, and cilantro to purée. Add the avocado and sour cream, processing just enough to combine. Season to taste with salt, pepper, and fresh lemon juice.

Rinse the scallions or onion with cold water to remove any bitter liquids. Stir onion and tomatoes in by hand.

When serving this as a salad or accompaniment to tortilla specialties, place a toasted tortilla chip in the center of the guacamole for garnish.

APPETIZERS AND SNACKS

There is no love sincerer than the love of food.
George Bernard Shaw

In Mexico, *antojitos* (snacks) are served as appetizers and are primarily tortilla or masa based. At some tables, partaking of these snacks can go on for hours and is followed by a late evening meal. While imitating this tradition is not recommended for a low-fat lifestyle, Mexican "snacks" for a party or for an afternoon of football are a sure winner.

Crisp or soft flautas and grilled anticuchos make perfect finger foods that are light on fat, rich in flavor. The many varieties of quesadillas are surprisingly low in calories and fun to serve with a choice of salsas. Mexican Party Dip is a lightened version of the popular layered dip made with beans, guacamole, and cheese, but this one won't send your daily fat gram count into orbit. By toasting tortillas instead of frying, cutting back on cheese and sour cream, and using fat-free products to give beans a creamy texture, you can enjoy these irresistible snacks more often.

◀ *Tortilla Pizzas: Shrimp and Guacamole, Black Bean and Chicken, and Chicken and Three Tomato Salsa* (Recipe on page 62)

Spicy Black Bean Dip With Melted Cheese

Serves
8

Fat grams
8

Calories
180

Very colorful and delicious with either crisp tortilla chips or toasted pita wedges.

The Beans:

1	16-ounce can black beans, drained
1/2	ounce low-fat smoked sausage, diced
1/2	cup minced onions
1/4	cup each minced red and green bell pepper
1	jalapeño chili, stemmed, seeded, and minced
1/4	cup chicken broth
1/2	teaspoon garlic salt
	Salt and pepper to taste

The Cheese:

2	ounces low-fat ricotta cheese
2	ounces low-fat Monterey Jack cheese, grated
4	ounces fat-free cream cheese
1	tablespoon Romano cheese, grated
1/4	teaspoon garlic salt
1/4	teaspoon cracked black pepper

The Tomatoes:

3–4	ripe Roma tomatoes, diced 1/4 inch
1	clove garlic, minced
1/2	tablespoon (more or less) safflower oil
1	tablespoon fresh basil or cilantro
	Salt and pepper to taste
	Tortilla Chips (p. 2)

To make the beans, drain the liquid from the can and set aside. Coat a small skillet generously with a vegetable spray and place over medium heat. Add sausage, garlic, onion, and bell pepper, tossing to prevent burning. Immediately add jalapeño and chicken broth (the mixture will sizzle) and reserved bean liquid. Simmer 5 to 6 minutes or until nearly all the liquid is absorbed. Add the beans and seasonings and cook 2 to 3 minutes or until hot.

To make the cheese, process the ricotta and Monterey Jack cheese until very smooth in a food processor fitted with the metal blade. Add remaining ingredients and process again. Spray a piece of aluminum foil with vegetable coating spray and press into an 8-ounce Pyrex cup, sprayed side up. Pack the cheese into the cup. When ready to serve, heat the cheese in a 350° oven for 10 minutes, then unmold on a large serving plate. Use a knife dipped in hot water to make the top smooth.

Put the tomatoes in a mixing bowl. Heat the safflower oil and garlic in a small skillet over medium heat. Cook 1 to 2 minutes to release flavor and soften garlic, but do not brown. Add the garlic to the tomatoes and season with basil or cilantro, salt, and pepper.

To serve, arrange the warm beans on one side of the cheese, the tomatoes on the other. Garnish the cheese with one tortilla chip in the center. Serve additional chips on the side.

CHILI CORNBREAD SQUARES

This variation on a tamale pie is a good addition to a buffet table or a tasty contribution when you have offered to "bring something." Great for tailgate parties or hearty appetizers.

*Makes
24 appetizer
squares, or
8 entrée servings*

*Fat grams
3
per square
10
per entrée serving*

*Calories
120 per square
358
per entrée serving*

1	pound top round, ground
2	cloves garlic, minced
4	teaspoons chili powder
1/2	cup diced green bell pepper
1/2	cup diced red bell pepper
1	onion, diced
1/2	teaspoon salt
1/4	teaspoon coarse ground black pepper
1/2	teaspoon coarse ground red chili flakes
1 1/2	cups stone ground cornmeal
1/2	cup all purpose flour
1	tablespoon sugar
4	teaspoons baking powder
	Egg substitute equivalent to 2 eggs
3/4	cups milk
1	16-ounce can creamed corn
2	teaspoons salt
2	jalapeño chilies, minced
4	ounces low-fat cheddar cheese, grated
2	tablespoons Parmesan cheese

Preheat the oven to 350°.

In a medium skillet, over medium heat, sauté the ground beef and garlic until lightly browned. Add the chili powder and stir to coat all the meat. Add the bell pepper, onion, and seasonings and cook, stirring occasionally, about 5 minutes. Remove and set aside.

Combine the dry ingredients in a bowl and mix well.

In a separate mixing bowl, beat the egg substitute with milk, creamed corn, salt, and chilies. Combine with the dry ingredients and mix well.

Spray a 9 × 13 casserole with a butter-flavored spray. Pour about two-thirds of the batter in the pan. Sprinkle evenly with the grated cheese. Top with the meat mixture, the remaining batter, and Parmesan cheese.

Bake for 40 to 45 minutes or until cornbread tests done. Cool about 10 minutes before cutting into squares.

Advance Preparation: This dish may be prepared a day in advance, baked, and then reheated when you are ready to serve. Chili Cornbread Squares also freeze quite well. Thaw completely before reheating.

Variation: Fat grams and calories may be cut further by using ground turkey in place of beef or by substituting a low-fat commercial chili (without beans) for the beef mixture for a "quick" version. In this case, if the chili has a moderately thin sauce, stir 1 to 2 tablespoons cornmeal into the warm chili to thicken.

Mexican Party
Dip

....

The ingredients in most versions of this popular dip can add up to a staggering amount of calories. In this recipe, calories and fat are trimmed from each layer, and the amount of cheese is minimized.

Serves
10

Fat grams
6

Calories
142

The Beans:

1/4	pound lean ground beef
2	cloves garlic minced
1	onion, chopped
1/4	cup minced green bell pepper
1 1/2	teaspoons chili powder
1	jalapeño chili, stemmed, seeded, minced
1/4	cup diced green chilies
1	16-ounce can pinto beans
4	tablespoons fat-free cream cheese
2–3	tablespoons picante sauce
	Salt and pepper to taste
4	ounce low-fat cheddar cheese, grated
	Skinny Guacamole (p. 39)
3/4	cups diced tomatoes

Garnish:

1 jalapeño chili, fresh or pickled, finely diced

Coat a medium skillet generously with a vegetable spray. Add the beef. Sear on medium high heat until browned. Add garlic, onion, bell pepper, chili powder, and chilies. Sauté, tossing constantly, 3 to 4 minutes.

Add the pinto beans and cream cheese. Cook 2 to 3 minutes or until combined. Transfer the mixture to a food processor fit-

◀ *Mexican Party Dip with Toasted Tortillas* (Recipe on page 47)

ted with the metal blade, add picante sauce, and process until puréed. Season with salt and pepper to taste. Spoon the beans into a 8-inch round plate.

Put half the grated cheese on top of the beans. Add guacamole on top of the cheese. Put remaining cheese around the edges, allowing the guacamole to be visible in the center. Arrange the tomatoes inside the cheese.

Garnish with diced chilies and serve with toasted tortilla chips (p. 2)

FLAUTAS

Flautas are crisp, little rolled tacos, sometimes called "taquitos." Soft Flautas are flour tortillas that are filled with cheese and chilies, rolled, and served with salsa. Crisp Flautas are filled with beef or chicken and are usually fried. Soft or crisp, flautas make wonderful little appetizers. Use very thin corn tortillas for flautas and bake them instead of frying to reduce fat calories.

Crisp Flautas

Serves
4

Fat grams
3 per flauta

Calories
120 per flauta

2	chicken breasts
12	corn tortillas
	Butter-flavored cooking spray
	Salt
4	cups thinly sliced leaf lettuce
	Skinny Guacamole (p. 39)
1	cup diced tomatoes

Shred the chicken meat and moisten with a small amount of chicken stock. Season with salt and pepper.

Soften the tortillas and place about 1 1/2 tablespoons shredded chicken in the center. Roll up tightly in a cigar shape and seal with two toothpicks.

Coat rolled tortillas on all sides with a butter-flavored cooking spray, sprinkle with salt, and place seam side down on a baking dish. Bake in a preheated 375° oven until crisp, about 20 minutes.

Serve flautas on a bed of thinly sliced lettuce with Skinny Guacamole and diced tomatoes, or arrange on a serving tray with Poblano Cream (p. 37) and picante sauce for dipping.

Soft Flautas

12	thin flour tortillas
8	ounces light cream cheese, softened
1	4 1/2-ounce can diced green chilies or
	2 poblano chilies, roasted, peeled, and diced
1/2	cup diced red and yellow bell peppers,
	roasted and peeled
	Beaten egg white

Serves
12

Fat grams
5 per flauta

Calories
112 per flauta

Soften the tortillas two at a time in a microwave oven.

Cream the cream cheese so it spreads easily. Spread each tortilla with about 1 1/2 ounces cream cheese. Evenly distribute the chilies and peppers on top. Brush the edges with egg white and roll up tightly like a cigar. Secure with 2 or 3 toothpicks. Place tortillas seam side down in a pan just large enough to accommodate all the tortillas. Wrap securely with plastic wrap and refrigerate for at least 3 hours.

Remove the toothpicks and serve the flautas with your favorite picante sauce.

Note: Fat grams can be reduced by more than half if using fat-free cream cheese.

ANTICUCHOS

Anticuchos are skewered pieces of beef, chicken, or shrimp that are marinated and grilled. These are fun to serve at a backyard barbecue with a variety of salsas.

The Marinade:

2	garlic cloves
3	serrano chilies, stemmed, seeded
1	cup cilantro leaves, packed
1	cup fresh lime juice
2	cups olive oil
1/2	cup white wine
2	teaspoons coarse salt
1 1/2	tablespoons red chili flakes

Put the garlic, serrano chilies, and cilantro in a blender jar and blend until diced. You may need to add some of the lime juice to aid blending. Remove and combine with remaining ingredients in a shallow bowl. Divide the marinade, using two-thirds for the shrimp and swordfish, one-third for the chicken.

	Wooden skewers
3	chicken breasts, boneless, skinless
1	pound shrimp, peeled, tails intact
10	ounces swordfish
	Poblano Cream (p. 37)
	Grilled Tomato Salsa (p. 26)
	Cilantro Cream (recipe follows)

Soak the skewers in hot water for 1 hour.

Trim fat from the chicken and cut into 3/4-inch square pieces. Remove skin and black portion of swordfish and cut into 3/4-inch pieces. Marinate shrimp and swordfish together, chicken separately, for 1 to 1 1/2 hours. Remove and skewer chicken, shrimp, and swordfish on separate skewers.

Preheat an outdoor grill with a hot fire. Remove skewered meats from the marinade and place on the grill. Season with salt and pepper and grill on both sides for about 5 minutes. Brush at least once with the marinade.

Serve Anticuchos with Poblano Cream (p. 37), Grilled Tomato Salsa (p. 26), and Cilantro Cream.

Cilantro Cream:

3	cloves fresh garlic
1/2	cup chopped cucumber
1	cup cilantro leaves, packed
1/3	cup chopped yellow bell pepper
1/4	cup chopped red bell pepper
4	ounces light cream cheese
	Fresh lime juice
	Salt and pepper to taste

Makes
1 cup

Fat grams
2 per tablespoon

Calories
20 per tablespoon

Using a blender or food processor fitted with the metal blade, process the garlic, cucumber, cilantro, and bell pepper with cream cheese until smooth. Season to taste with lime juice, salt, and pepper.

MUSHROOM
TORTAS

Makes
8

Fat grams
3

Calories
156

Almost any combination of mushrooms may be used. Wild mushrooms have more intense flavors, but you may use domestic, brown, or shitake with excellent results. The same filling may be used in soft tacos with flour tortillas, enchiladas using cornmeal crepes, or corn tortilla cups in place of the rolls. Instructions for making the tortilla cups are on p. 3

8	small French rolls, oval shaped
1–2	tablespoons safflower oil
1/2	red onion, diced
1	large clove garlic, minced
8	ounces domestic mushrooms, cleaned, quartered
8	ounces shitake mushrooms, cleaned, sliced
8	ounces brown mushrooms, cleaned quartered
1	red bell pepper, roasted, peeled, chopped
1/2–1	tablespoon chipotle, liquid only
3	tablespoons tomato sauce
	Salt and pepper to taste
1	tablespoon fresh minced basil
1	tablespoon fresh minced parsley
	Feta cheese or Crema (p. 21)
	Sprigs of fresh basil or parsley, with stem

Preheat the oven to broil.

Cut a thin slice from the top of each roll. Pull away and discard part of the soft center portion from each roll, making a cavity for the mushrooms. Spray both top and inside of roll generously with a butter-flavored spray and place on a cookie sheet. Broil on the top rack, watching closely, to toast the inside. Remove and set aside.

Heat the safflower oil over medium heat in a large skillet. Add onion, garlic, and mushrooms and sauté over medium heat until lightly browned and softened, about 5 to 8 minutes. Add red bell pepper and chipotle, starting with the lesser amount first. (Chipotle is fire-hot so add, taste, and decide whether to add the full amount). Season with salt, pepper, and fresh herbs.

Spoon the mushrooms into the warm toasted rolls, allowing mushrooms to spill onto each plate.

Garnish with crumbled feta cheese or a spoonful of Crema. Serve the toasted roll "top" on the side.

Enchiladas: Fill 8 enchiladas as directed on page 137. Use Mild Tomato Enchilada Sauce (p. 140), shredded lettuce and garnish with crumbled feta cheese, goat cheese, or light sour cream.

Tortilla Cups: Prepare 8 corn or flour tortilla cups according to the directions on page 3. Spoon filling into each one, and top with cheese or light sour cream.

Caramel Crepes with Caramel Sauce (Recipes on pages 184 and 188)

Shrimp and Scallop Ceviche

Serves
8

Fat grams
6

Calories
189

Ceviche is usually made from raw fish that is cooked by enzymes in lime juice. In this method, the shellfish are poached before being marinated. You may use any combination of fish and shellfish; however, the fish must be fresh, not frozen. This makes a very light, refreshing appetizer.

1	pound fresh shrimp, peeled, tails removed, cut in thirds (51–60 count)
1/2	pound fresh bay scallops, halved
	White wine
	Water
	Peppercorns
1	onion, sliced
1 1/2	cups fresh lime juice
2	garlic cloves, minced
1	cup fresh cilantro, stemmed (loosely packed)
2	serrano chilies, stemmed, seeded
2	tablespoons safflower oil
1/2	teaspoon salt
1/8	teaspoon white pepper
1	cup fresh tomatoes, diced
6	leaves Boston or Bibb lettuce
6	cilantro sprigs

Garnish:

Mango and avocado (optional)
Tortilla strips (p. 2)

Bring equal amounts of water and white wine to a boil in a saucepan. Add onion, peppercorns, shrimp, and scallops. As soon as water returns to a boil, cover and remove from the heat. Let stand 6 to 10 minutes, then strain and cool.

When completely cool, place the shellfish in a shallow container and add the lime juice. Cover and refrigerate 2 to 3 hours.

In a blender or food processor fitted with the metal blade, combine the garlic, cilantro, and serrano chilies and blend well. Add the oil and blend to combine. Add the blended cilantro mixture to the shellfish and mix in well. Season to taste with salt and pepper.

When ready to serve, pour off most of the lime juice and add fresh tomatoes. Serve the ceviche in lettuce leaves and garnish with fresh cilantro sprigs.

Garnish each plate with a slice of avocado and mango and a few crisp tortilla chips.

QUESADILLAS

Southwesterners have quickly abandoned the traditional Mexican method of preparing quesadillas. I suspect we like our fat hidden. In the old method, corn tortillas were filled with cheese and fried in oil, resulting in a tasty but greasy quesadilla. Today most quesadillas are prepared with flour tortillas and may be "stacked" or folded before they are toasted on a hot griddle. A nonstick frying pan or griddle works very well to brown the quesadillas. To be sure the fillings are hot, bake them in a preheated oven 5 to 10 minutes after browning.

Quesadillas may be as simple as melted cheese, onions, and green chilies, or try one of the combinations that follow. The procedure for Roasted Pepper and Onion Quesadillas is the same as for Crab Quesadillas. Restaurant chefs give free rein to their imaginations, so don't be surprised to find everything from smoked duck to wild mushroom quesadillas on popular menus.

Quesadillas may be prepared 6 to 8 hours in advance. Wrap them in plastic wrap and refrigerate until you are ready to cook.

Crab Quesadillas

*30 wedges as an appetizer
(2 per person)*

*Fat grams
3.5*

*Calories
108*

The fresh lump crabmeat from the Texas Coast is delicious with spicy chilies. Serve these with your favorite picante sauce and the Poblano Cream on p 37. One of my testers prepared these using an imitation crab product and was very pleased with the results.

1	pound lump crabmeat
1	cup chopped onion
1/3	cup each, diced red and green bell peppers
3	tablespoons diced (pickled) jalapeño chilies
2	ounces fat-free cream cheese
2	tablespoons light mayonnaise
2	teaspoons fresh lemon juice
1	tablespoon fresh minced parsley
	Salt and pepper to taste
10	flour tortillas
1	cup fresh diced tomatoes
5	ounces low-fat Monterey Jack cheese or 5 slices non-fat Swiss cheese

Pick over the crabmeat, removing any small bones or cartilage.

Coat a nonstick skillet with vegetable spray and place over medium heat. Sauté onion and bell pepper 1 to 2 minutes to soften. Add jalapeño chilies and cream cheese. Remove from heat and stir the cheese to mix in the cream cheese. In a small bowl, mix the mayonnaise, lemon juice, and parsley. Gently stir in the crabmeat and season to taste with salt and pepper.

Soften flour tortillas 2 or 3 at a time. Spread the crabmeat mixture in the center and fold over. Press down firmly. Open again and top one half the tortilla with diced tomatoes and about 1/2 ounce cheese. Fold and set aside. Prepare remaining tortillas.

When ready to cook the quesadillas, preheat the oven to 350°. Place a nonstick skillet over medium heat and cook quesadillas until lightly browned on both sides. Reduce the heat if they brown too rapidly. Transfer to a cookie sheet and finish baking in the oven 4 to 5 minutes. Cut in wedges and serve with Poblano Cream and a mild tomato salsa or one of the fruit salsas on pages 31, 32, and 33.

Roasted Pepper and Onion Quesadillas

1/2	yellow onion, halved and cut in thin strips
1	yellow bell pepper, in short julienne strips
1	red bell pepper, in short julienne strips
2	poblano chilies, roasted, peeled, diced
1	papaya, peeled and diced
10	3/4-ounce slices nonfat Swiss cheese
10	flour tortillas

*30 wedges as an
appetizer
(2 per person)*

*Fat grams
3*

*Calories
89*

Coat a medium skillet with a vegetable spray and place over medium heat. Add onion and bell peppers and sauté until softened and lightly browned, about 2 to 3 minutes. Season with salt and pepper and set aside.

Combine papaya and poblano chilies. Soften the tortillas 2 to 3 at a time. Assemble in the following manner: put one-tenth the onion mixture on half the tortilla, one-tenth the papaya-chili mixture followed by 1 slice Swiss cheese. Fold over and press down firmly. Repeat until all the tortillas have been filled.

Cook tortillas according to the method described in Crab Quesadillas. Serve with Jicama Salsa (p. 35) or light sour cream.

Spinach/Mushroom Quesadillas

16–20 pieces

Fat grams 14 per whole quesadilla (4–5 pieces)

Calories 252 per whole quesadilla (4–5 pieces)

Quesadillas are great for snacks or appetizers. Any low-fat or no-fat cheese may be used or omit the cheese completely. In this version the quesadillas are stacked rather than folded.

2	cloves garlic, minced
8	mushrooms, thinly sliced
1/2	cup diced yellow onion

Preheat the oven to 300°.

Coat a medium skillet with a nonstick vegetable spray. Over medium heat sauté the garlic, mushrooms, and half the onions. Turn often, cooking quickly. Season with salt and pepper and set aside.

1/4	cup diced red bell pepper
1/2	cup diced green chilies
1	10-ounce package frozen spinach, thawed and well drained
3	ounces light or low-fat cream cheese, at room temperature
1/2–1	teaspoon salt (to taste)
1/8	teaspoon cayenne pepper
1	tablespoon Parmesan cheese
1/2	cup chunky-style picante sauce
6	ounces low-fat Monterey Jack or cheddar cheese, grated
8	flour tortillas, 5–6 inches in diameter

Garnish:

Pico de Gallo (p. 24)

Rinse the pan, and using the same method, sauté the remaining onion, bell pepper, and chilies. Stir in the spinach, cream cheese, salt, cayenne pepper, and Parmesan cheese.

To assemble the tortillas, divide the spinach mixture evenly on 4 tortillas. Spread to within 1/2 inch of the edge. Top with the mushrooms, picante sauce, and grated cheese. Put the remaining 4 tortillas on top and press down firmly.

Coat a clean skillet with vegetable spray and place over medium heat. Cook quesadillas briefly on both sides to brown, then transfer to a cookie sheet and place in the oven to keep warm while cooking the remaining tortillas.

Cut quesadillas in quarters or wedges for serving.

Garnish with Pico de Gallo.

NACHOS

Nachos come in many shapes, sizes, and varieties from individual tortillas topped with beans and melted cheese to "ball park" nachos where a melted cheese sauce tops a plate of tortillas. If you toast the tortillas, use fat-free beans and low-fat cheese. You'll cut both fat and calories substantially. I've outlined several techniques for preparing nachos and suggested toppings.

Individual Bean Nachos

1	corn tortilla, toasted
2	tablespoons mashed beans (p. 19)
1 1/2	ounces low-fat cheddar cheese, grated

Garnish:

4	pickled jalapeño chilies
	Picante sauce

*Makes
2 servings*

*Fat grams
4*

*Calories
102*

Spray the tortilla on both sides with a butter-flavored spray and sprinkle lightly with salt. Place on a baking sheet and bake at 350° for 10 minutes or until crisp.

Preheat the oven to broil.

Spread the tortilla with mashed beans and top with cheese. Place on the highest oven rack. Broil about 1 minute, or until cheese melts. Using a sharp knife, cut the tortilla into 4 pieces.

Garnish nachos with jalapeño chilies and serve with picante sauce.

Ball Park Nachos

Serves
4

Fat grams
8

Calories
217

8	corn tortillas, quartered and toasted
	Queso (p.38)
1/2	cup Pico de Gallo (p. 24)

Prepare the tortilla chips and mound on an oval, heat-proof plate. Prepare the Queso, and pour hot Queso over the tortilla chips.

Serve with Pico de Gallo on top.

Smoked Chicken Nachos

Makes
2 servings

Fat grams
5

Calories
135

1	corn tortilla, toasted
3	tablespoons mashed black beans (p. 19)
2	ounces smoked chicken, shredded
2	tablespoons diced tomatoes
1 1/2	ounces low-fat Monterey Jack cheese, grated

Garnish:

Pickled jalapeño chilies

Spread the beans on the toasted tortilla. Top with smoked chicken, tomatoes, and Monterey Jack cheese.

Heat as directed under the broiling element.

Cut in quarters and top each one with jalapeños.

San Antonio Nachos

Makes
2 servings

Fat grams
5–7

Calories
145–160

1	corn tortilla toasted
3	tablespoons mashed pinto beans (p. 19)
2	ounces chicken or beef fajita meat, diced
1 1/2	ounces low-fat Monterey Jack cheese, grated

Garnish:

| 4 | tablespoons Skinny Guacamole (p. 39) |
| 2 | tablespoons diced tomatoes |

Spread the beans on the toasted tortilla. Top with chicken or beef and Monterey Jack cheese.

Heat as directed under the broiling element.

Cut into quarters and garnish each quarter with guacamole and diced tomatoes.

Shrimp Nachos

1/2	cup diced red onion
6	ounces chopped shrimp
	Salt and pepper
1/2	teaspoon chili powder
2	teaspoons minced cilantro
8	corn tortillas, quartered and toasted
	Queso (p. 38)
1/2	cup Pico de Gallo (p. 24)

Serves
4

Fat grams
8

Calories
290

Coat a medium skillet with a vegetable spray and place over medium heat. Add onion and shrimp, season with salt and pepper and sauté 1 to 2 minutes or until shrimp turns pink. Stir in chili powder and cilantro.

Evenly distribute the shrimp over toasted tortillas. Top with warm, melted Queso and Pico de Gallo.

Taco Nachos

1	cup Taco Meat (p. 128)
8	corn tortillas, quartered and toasted
	Queso (p. 38)
1/2	cup Pico de Gallo

Serves
4

Fat grams
12

Calories
297

Prepare the Taco Meat. Evenly distribute warm meat over the toasted tortilla chips.

Top with warm Queso and garnish with Pico de Gallo.

TORTILLA PIZZAS

*Serves
1*

Often called "tostaditos," these mini snacks are a cross between a small chalupa and round nacho. You may use flour or corn tortillas as a base or small pita rounds. Hot or cold, they make good appetizers at a party with a variety of toppings. The general procedure follows, along with some of my favorite combinations.

> Corn or flour tortillas, 3 inches in diameter, or
> pita rounds, halved, 3 inches in diameter
> Butter-flavored spray
> Salt

Preheat the oven to 350°.

Cut tortillas into 3-inch rounds. Coat both sides with butter-flavored spray and sprinkle lightly with salt. Bake on a cookie sheet for 8 minutes or until crisp.

Cold Toppings

*For
1 tortilla*

*Fat grams
1*

*Calories
50*

1	tablespoon Skinny Guacamole (p. 39)
1	cooked shrimp
	Picante sauce or Mango Salsa (p. 31)

Spread the guacamole on the toasted tortilla. Season the shrimp with salt and pepper and place on top. Garnish with salsa of choice.

*Fat grams
1*

*Calories
62*

1	tablespoon Spicy Bean Dip (p. 36) or Chunky Salsa (p. 28)
1	tablespoon light sour cream
	Shredded Romaine lettuce

Spread the tortilla with Spicy Bean Dip. Top with salsa, sour cream, and shredded lettuce.

Hot Toppings

2	tablespoons shredded, seasoned chicken	*For*
1	slice avocado	*1 tortilla*
1	tablespoon Three Tomato Salsa or	
	Mango Salsa (p. 31)	*Fat grams*
		1.5

Calories
55

Heat the chicken in a small skillet. Place on a warm tortilla and top with avocado and salsa.

2	tablespoons Taco Meat (p. 128)	*Fat grams*
1	teaspoon light sour cream	*4*
	Shredded lettuce	
1/4	ounce crumbled feta cheese	*Calories*
	Diced jalapeño chilies	*85*

Heat the Taco Meat in a small skillet. Top with sour cream, lettuce, feta cheese, and jalapeño chilies.

1/2	ounce grilled diced chicken seasoned	*Fat grams*
1	tablespoon Poblano Cream (p. 37)	*2*
1	slice Roma tomato	
1	teaspoon light sour cream	*Calories*
	Sliced lettuce	*55*
	Crumbled feta cheese	

Heat the grilled chicken in a small skillet coated with vegetable oil. Season with salt and pepper. Put the cream on the tortilla and top with chicken, tomato slice, sour cream, lettuce and, cheese.

TOSTADA GRANDE

Serves
16

Fat grams
7

Calories
208

This recipe will remind you of a giant quesadilla or stacked enchilada. Cut it into wedges or squares and serve it on a pizza stone for a Mexican buffet.

3	burrito-sized flour tortillas
1	cup Mashed Black Beans (p. 19)
1 1/2	cups shredded smoked or barbecued chicken
1/4	teaspoon chili powder
2	ounces fat-free cream cheese
1/2	cup low-fat ricotta cheese
	Salt and pepper
2	tablespoons Romano cheese
1	cup diced onion
1	4 1/2-ounce can diced green chilies
1	tablespoon light butter
2	ounces low-fat cheddar cheese, grated
1 1/2	cups thinly sliced Romaine or red-tip leaf lettuce
1 1/2	cups diced tomatoes
3	ounces crumbled feta cheese

Preheat the oven to 350°.

Place flour tortillas directly on the rack and bake 4 minutes to toast. Tortillas will not be crisp.

Coat a pizza pan or pizza stone with vegetable coating spray. Put one tortilla on the pan and top with mashed beans and chicken. Sprinkle with salt, pepper, and chili powder. Top with the second tortilla.

Combine the cream cheese, ricotta, and Romano cheese in a food processor fitted with the metal blade. Season with salt and pepper and spread on top of the second tortilla.

Heat a small skillet over medium heat and sauté the chilies and onion in butter until softened, about 2 minutes. Put on top of the cheese mixture. Put the third tortilla on top of the chilies. Press down firmly.

Bake for 10 minutes, then top with grated cheese and bake 5 to 10 minutes.

Top with the lettuce and tomato. Drizzle with cream and top with crumbled feta cheese.

TORTILLA ROLL UPS

A colorful variation of a soft flauta, this appetizer can be sliced diagonally and served with a mild tomato salsa.

1/4	cup Green Chili Pesto (p. 20)
6	ounces nonfat cream cheese, softened
	Salt and pepper
8	flour tortillas
1 1/2	cups Black Bean Salsa (variation on p. 24)

Using a fork, combine the Green Chili Pesto with the cream cheese.

Soften the tortillas and spread each one with the cream cheese mixture. Season with salt and pepper. Drain the salsa well and place it in the center of each tortilla. Roll tortillas tightly and secure them with a toothpick. Chill, covered with plastic wrap until ready to serve.

To serve, slice each one on the diagonal and secure slices with a toothpick.

Makes 8

Fat grams
3.5 (5 pieces)

Calories
146 (5 pieces)

SALADS

In the past, Mexican restaurants have used lettuces to garnish combination plates, and salads have been limited to Taco Salads, which can weigh in heavy on fat and calories—some in excess of 900 calories and 60 fat grams. Today, Mexican restaurants have expanded their salad selections to include Caesar Salads and salads made with fajita chicken and shrimp.

This section calls for fresh fruits and vegetables and a variety of beans to create a number of colorful and delicious salads that can be accompaniments as well as entrées. Studies have shown that many people consume more fat grams and calories from salad dressings, mayonnaise, and cheese than any other food, so there are some significant savings to be found here. Vinaigrettes are lightened, cheese is limited or low-fat, and flavors and textures are emphasized by using fruits, vegetables, and oven-fried tortilla strips. You'll find light versions of your favorite beef and chicken taco salad, Caesar Salad, as well as Smoked Turkey Salad, Tequila Orange Salad, and a colorful, spicy Southwestern Bean Salad.

◀ *Crisp Flautas with Skinny Guacamole (Recipes on pages 48 and 39)*

Tequila-Orange Salad

This is a very light, refreshing salad that goes well with spicy foods.

Serves 5

Fat grams 9

Calories 270

1	large head red-tip leaf lettuce
4	seedless oranges, sectioned, juice reserved

Tequila-Orange Vinaigrette

1	ounce tequila
1/4	cup reserved orange juice
1	tablespoon orange juice concentratate
1 1/2	ounces triple sec (or any orange liqueur)
1	clove garlic
1 1/2	teaspoons Dijon mustard
	Pinch sugar
3	tablespoons rice wine vinegar
4–5	tablespoons safflower oil
1/2	teaspoon salt
1/8	teaspoon white pepper or cayenne pepper
2	sprigs fresh parsley
1	cup red bell pepper, roasted, peeled and cut into short julienne strips
1 1/2	cups jicama, cut into short julienne strips
4	corn tortillas, in thin strips, toasted (p. 2)

Garnish

1–1 1/2	cups fresh, diced tomatoes
4	ounces crumbled cotija or feta cheese

Rinse lettuce thoroughly and shake to remove all moisture. Dry on paper towels. Cut the lettuce into bite-sized pieces and refrigerate in zip-lock bags lined with paper towels for 2 hours.

To section the oranges, cut off both ends and discard. Use a sharp knife to cut away the peel and membrane. Cut between sections to remove perfect wedges. Squeeze the juice from remaining pulp and reserve.

Put the tequila, reserved orange juice, orange juice concentrate, and triple sec in a small saucepan and bring to a boil. Boil 3 to 4 minutes until reduced by about one-third the volume.

Into a blender jar, place the garlic, mustard, and reduced orange mixture. Blend until smooth. Add the sugar, vinegar, oil, salt, and white pepper. Blend again. Add parsley and blend briefly to chop the parsley.

Toss the chilled lettuce with bell peppers, jicama, orange sections, radishes, and dressing. Divide among 5 serving plates.

Top with tortilla strips. Garnish with diced tomatoes and crumbled cheese

Advance Preparation: The lettuces may be rinsed and chilled a day in advance. The dressing and salad ingredients may be prepared in advance.

SPINACH CORN SALAD

Serves
5

Fat grams
12

Calories
241

This is another light salad that is delicious with the Tequila Orange Vinaigrette. You can use jicama in place of the red bell peppers or a mixture of baby lettuces in place of the spinach.

1	pound fresh, young spinach, rinsed
2	red bell peppers, roasted, peeled, and cut into short strips
1 1/2	cups fresh corn kernels, blanched
3	ounces feta or mild goat cheese, crumbled
	Tequila Orange Vinaigrette (p. 68)
	Cracked black pepper
	Fresh lime wedge
2	corn tortillas, in thin strips, toasted

Cut the spinach into bite-size pieces and toss with the roasted peppers, corn, cheese, and vinaigrette.

Divide the salad between 5 serving plates. Garnish each one with cracked black pepper, lime wedges, and tortilla strips.

CAESAR SALAD

Traditional Caesar salads can be laden with hidden fat. In this version, fat and calories have been trimmed by more than half. Try the shrimp and chicken variations at the end of the recipe, and you can make one of the most popular restaurant salads at home, with half the fat and calories.

Serves
5

Fat grams
19

Calories
400
(Without shrimp or chicken)

With chicken
Fat grams
22
Calories
508

With shrimp
Fat grams
21
Calories
514

1	large head Romaine lettuce
1	cup fresh corn kernels
1	cup diced tomatoes, preferably Roma
2	ounces grated Parmesan or Romano cheese

The Dressing:

1	garlic clove
1/2	teaspoon anchovy paste
1	tablespoon Worcestershire sauce
2	teaspoons Dijon mustard
	Juice from 1 lemon
2	tablespoons balsamic or sherry vinegar
2	tablespoons grated Romano cheese
1/2	teaspoon salt
	Pinch white pepper
4	tablespoons safflower oil
1	egg white

The Croutons:

6	slices French bread
1	teaspoon salt
1	teaspoon coarsely ground black pepper
1/2	teaspoon cayenne pepper
1	tablespoon Parmesan or Romano cheese, finely ground

Optional:

1	pound fresh shrimp, cooked or
4	chicken breasts, grilled and cut into bite-sized pieces

Rinse and dry the lettuce thoroughly. Cut leaves down the center rib and chop into bite-sized pieces. Store the lettuce in plastic bags lined with paper towel.

To prepare the dressing, put the garlic, anchovy paste, mustard, and lemon juice in a blender jar or food processor fitted with the metal blade and blend smooth. Add the cheese, salt, and pepper. While the blender runs, pour the oil and egg white through the top. Set aside.

Preheat the oven to 450°. Cut the bread into small cubes about 1/4 to 1/2 inch square and put them in a mixing bowl. Combine the salt, pepper, and Parmesan cheese. Generously coat the bread cubes with a butter-flavored spray, sprinkle with seasoning, and toss. Repeat to coat all the croutons and place on a cookie sheet. Bake 5 to 6 minutes or until lightly browned.

When you are ready to serve the salad, drop the corn kernels in boiling salted water for 1 minute to blanch. Refresh in ice water. Toss the chilled Romaine lettuce with the corn, croutons, tomatoes, and dressing.

Divide the salad between 4 salad plates and garnish with cheese.

Shrimp or Chicken Variations: If preparing a Shrimp or Chicken Caesar, cook the shrimp or chicken ahead. Toss with the greens and place 4–5 pieces on top after tossing the salad.

Advance Preparation: The lettuce, dressing, and croutons may be prepared a day ahead.

WANDA'S CORN
SALAD

Serves
8

Fat grams
5

Calories
186

My friend Wanda Wheatly served this salad at a casual dinner party, and it was a tremendous hit with both the men and women. Any "healthy" recipe that has this much appeal is a winner. Because this salad is best made a day ahead, it is a perfect dish for summer entertaining or to accompany grilled meats, chicken, or fish.

3	11-ounce cans white corn
1	large cucumber, peeled, seeded and diced
2	large tomatoes, chopped
2	small green bell peppers, chopped
1	4 1/2-ounce can diced green chilies
1	red onion, chopped
2	teaspoons salt
1/2	teaspoon pepper
1/2	teaspoon celery seed
3	tablespoons light mayonnaise
2	tablespoons sour cream
2	tablespoons rice wine vinegar

Combine the corn, cucumber, tomatoes, bell peppers, chilies, and red onion in a large bowl. Season with salt, pepper, and celery seed.

Combine the mayonnaise, sour cream, and vinegar in a small mixing bowl. Toss with the vegetables and refrigerate, covered, overnight.

SOUTHWESTERN
BEAN SALAD

Use whatever vegetables, beans, or combination of beans and vegetables that appeal to you or are fresh and seasonal. Black beans make a substantial base and give the salad wonderful color contrast.

Serves
8

Fat grams
15

Calories
392

The Dressing:

3	garlic cloves
5	tablespoons fresh lime or lemon juice
1	serrano chili, stemmed and seeded (optional)
2	tablespoons vinegar
1	teaspoon Dijon mustard
	Pinch sugar
1/2	cup safflower oil
2	sprigs fresh parsley
1	sprig fresh mint
1/2	teaspoon oregano
1/2	teaspoon salt
1	15-ounce can black beans, drained
1	bunch scallions, sliced (green and white part)
1 1/2	cups diced jicama
1 1/2	cups fresh corn kernels, blanched
1	cup chopped red bell pepper
1	cup cooked pinto or garbanzo beans
1/2	cup diced papaya or mango, firm
	Salt and pepper to taste

To make the dressing, place the garlic in a blender jar and blend to mince. Add the lime or lemon juice and serrano chili and blend again. Add remaining ingredients and blend smooth.

Combine the beans, scallions, jicama, corn, pepper, pinto or garbanzo beans, and papaya or mango in a bowl. Toss well and adjust salt and pepper to taste. Refrigerate for 4 to 5 hours before serving.

Sweet and Spicy Slaw

Makes
8 servings

Fat grams
trace

Calories
81

1	small head white cabbage, thinly sliced
1	tablespoon juice from pickled jalapeños
1/4	cup sugar
1/2	cup white wine vinegar
1/4	cup water
1	cup jicama, in short julienne strips
1	green bell pepper, julienne strips
1	red bell pepper, julienne strips
1	yellow bell pepper, julienne strips
1	granny smith apple, unpeeled, in julienne strips
1	cup shredded carrots
	Salt and pepper to taste

Put the cabbage in a 9 × 13 casserole dish. Bring jalapeño juice, sugar, vinegar, and water to a boil. Pour over cabbage and let marinate for 2 to 3 hours, refrigerated.

Transfer the cabbage to a large bowl and add jicama, bell peppers, apples, and carrots. Toss to coat all ingredients. Season to taste with salt and pepper.

GRILLED CHICKEN
SALAD

....

This entrée salad is best prepared in individual servings rather than a large bowl. It makes a perfect summer supper or lunch entrée.

Serves
5

Fat grams
16

Calories
436

The Marinade:

1	bottle prepared Italian dressing
2	tablespoons soy sauce
3	cloves fresh minced garlic
3	serrano chilies, chopped
10	boneless, skinless chicken breasts
1/2	head iceberg lettuce, thinly sliced
1/2	head Romaine lettuce, chopped bite-sized
1/2	head leaf lettuce, chopped bite-sized
1	large onion, julienne strips
1	red bell pepper, julienne strips
1	yellow bell pepper, julienne strips
1	green bell pepper, julienne strips
3	flour tortillas, toasted
2	ounces low-fat Monterey Jack cheese, grated
2	ounces low-fat Cheddar Cheese, grated
	Fat-free Ranch Dressing
	Picante Sauce

Three or four hours in advance, combine the marinade ingredients and marinate the chicken breasts.

When ready to prepare the salad, heat an outdoor grill to the highest setting. Remove chicken from the marinade and season on both sides with salt and pepper. Grill the chicken until well marked and the edges take on a "cooked" appearance, about 4 to 5 minutes. Turn to grill the opposite side for 3 or 4 minutes, depending on the thickness of the chicken.

Combine the cleaned lettuces and divide among four dinner plates.

Coat a large skillet with a vegetable spray and place over medium heat. Add onions and peppers and sauté until lightly browned. You will have to use additional spray to prevent burning, and toss peppers frequently. Put onions and peppers on top of the greens and toss with lettuces.

Preheat the oven to broil. Put toasted tortillas on a cookie sheet and sprinkle with both cheeses. Broil on the top rack a few minutes until cheese melts. Cut the tortillas in 6 wedges and put around the edges of the plates. Slice the chicken breast diagonally with a sharp knife, cutting each breast into 4 or 5 slices. Arrange on top of the salad.

Serve the salads with Ranch Dressing and Picante Sauce.

TACO SALAD

Serves
4

Beef

Fat grams
26
Calories
625

Chicken

Fat grams
19
Calories
586

Serve this popular salad in flour tortilla "bowls" or layer it in a 2-quart bowl and serve on a buffet table. Either way, you will not miss a salad dressing, which can run up the calories and fat grams.

1/2	head iceberg lettuce
1	small head Romaine lettuce or leaf lettuce
1	16-ounce can pinto beans
1	cup chopped onion
2	cups diced tomatoes
	Skinny Guacamole (p. 39)
3	ounces low-fat cheddar or Monterey Jack cheese, grated
2 1/2	cups cooked chicken, well-seasoned or Taco Meat (p. 128)
8	corn tortillas, in strips, toasted

Clean lettuces and cut into bite-sized pieces. Dry thoroughly and place in paper towel lined zip-lock bags. Refrigerate to "crisp" lettuces. Drain pinto beans and reserve the liquid. Season the beans with salt and pepper. Sear the onion in a small skillet seasoned with vegetable spray over medium heat.

Remove and stir in 3 to 4 tablespoons of the bean liquid. Toss with the pinto beans.

To assemble the salad, put about half the lettuce in a bowl. Scatter two-thirds of the bean mixture on top, half the tomatoes on top of the beans, then half of the guacamole and tortilla strips. Sprinkle with cheddar cheese. Repeat with a second layer in this order: all the chicken, guacamole, beans, and tortilla strips. Arrange remaining cheese around the edge of the bowl.

Taco Bowl Preparation: Prepare the bowl as directed on p. 3. Toss the lettuces with the beans and place them in the tortilla bowl. Arrange chicken, grated cheese, and tomatoes on top. Put guacamole in the center. Place the tortilla bowl on a bed of sliced lettuce and a few tortilla strips.

Tortilla Salad

Serves
6

Fat grams
34

Calories
578

Prepare this salad with shrimp or chicken. The dressing is light, and you need very little because the fresh fruits and tortillas supply a variety of flavor and textures. The Poblano Cream gives just a hint of spice for fun. The fat grams and calories are significantly less without the avocado.

Lemon Garlic Vinaigrette:

1	clove garlic
2	tablespoons lemon juice
2	tablespoons lime juice
1	tablespoon honey
2	tablespoons white wine vinegar
1	tablespoon Dijon mustard
1/3	cup safflower oil
1/2	teaspoon salt
1/4	teaspoon white pepper
1	egg white
3–4	sprigs parsley
1	head red-tip leaf lettuce
1/2	head Romaine lettuce
1	cup very thinly sliced red cabbage or radicchio
6	chicken breasts, grilled
1	red bell pepper, in short strips
1	papaya, peeled and diced
1 1/2	cup diced tomatoes
1	small avocado, diced
8	corn tortillas in thin strips, toasted
1/4	cup Poblano Cream (p. 37)

Put the garlic, lemon, and lime juice in the blender and blend to mince the garlic. Add honey, vinegar, and mustard and blend smooth. While the blender runs, add the oil, salt, pepper, egg white, and parsley. Adjust seasonings to taste.

Rinse and thoroughly dry the lettuces. Toss together in a large bowl.

Slice grilled chicken in short julienne strips and season with salt and pepper. Toss chicken, bell pepper, papaya, tomato, avocado, half the tortilla strips, and lettuces with the dressing. Divide the salad between six serving plates.

Garnish each plate with additional tortilla strips in the center of each salad. Put the Poblano Cream in a zip-lock bag and snip the square edge with scissors. Drizzle on top of each salad.

Advance Preparation: The chicken and the dressing may be prepared a day in advance. The avocado and papaya may be cut 3 or 4 hours in advance and refrigerated with the dressing.

PASTA SALAD WITH CHICKEN AND CILANTRO

This light salad may be prepared 2-3 hours in advance. Coat the cooked pasta with an olive oil spray to prevent it from sticking together. Always check seasoning on pasta salads prior to service as the pasta tends to neutralize the seasonings.

Serves 4

Fat grams 14

Calories 317

2	cups cooked penne, macaroni, or rotelle pasta
3	grilled chicken breasts, diced
1	cup diced tomatoes
1	4 1/2-ounce can diced green chilies
1/3	cup fresh cilantro leaves
	Lemon Garlic Vinaigrette (p. 78)
1	cup cooked black beans, well drained
4	cups thinly sliced Romaine lettuce

Toss the pasta with chicken, tomatoes, green chilies, cilantro, and vinaigrette.

Drain the beans and discard any broken ones. Gently toss the beans with the pasta. Season to taste with salt and pepper.

Serve the salad atop thinly sliced Romaine lettuce.

Smoked Turkey Salad

Serves
6

Fat grams
16.5

Calories
458

This is my favorite entrée salad. I have prepared it with a variety of smoked meats, from duck to pheasant. It is very colorful and light and may be served as an entrée luncheon salad for 5 or 6 or an appetizer salad for 8 people. The different flavors, textures, and slightly spicy vinaigrette make an attractive, interesting combination.

| 1 | head Boston or Bibb lettuce |
| 1 | bunch watercress or arugula |

The Dressing:

1/2	cup rich chicken broth or Smoked Turkey Stock (p. 15) (see note)
1/2	cup white wine
2	shallots, minced
2	teaspoons Dijon mustard
1	tablespoon fresh lemon juice
1	serrano chili, stemmed, seeded
1	egg white
1	teaspoon salt
	Pinch sugar
4	tablespoons safflower oil

1	small jicama (about 4 ounces)
1	red bell pepper, in short julienne strips
1	yellow bell pepper, in short julienne strips
6	ounces French beans (*haricots verte*)
2	carrots, peeled, blanched and cut in julienne strips
1 1/4–1 1/2	pound smoked turkey, breast meat, in julienne strips
1/2	cup black beans, well seasoned
2	each, red and yellow corn tortillas, in thin strips, toasted (p. 2)

Core Boston lettuce and separate into leaves. Rinse and dry thoroughly. Chill until ready to use. Stem and rinse watercress or arugula.

To make the dressing, bring the chicken broth, wine, and shallots to a boil in a small saucepan. Boil 3 to 4 minutes or until reduced by about half. Put shallots in a blender jar and add mustard, lemon juice, and serrano chili. Blend smooth. With the blender running, add the egg white, salt, sugar, and safflower oil. Set aside.

Cut all the vegetables and turkey into strips about 2 1/2 inches in length. Toss meat, vegetables, and dressing together.

Arrange Boston lettuce leaves on six serving plates. Place watercress or arugula on top of the Boston lettuce. Toss half the tortilla strips with the meat and vegetables just before serving. Mound the mixture on top of the greens. Garnish with a few black beans and tortilla strips.

Note: A rich stock like the Smoked Turkey Stock on page 13 adds a great deal of flavor to this dish. To make a quick version, use meaty bones from a turkey or chicken and place in about 2 cups of canned chicken broth. Boil for about 30 minutes, then cool the broth with the bones in the broth. Strain the stock and refrigerate. Skim all fat. Use 1/4 cup in the dressing.

SOUPS, STEWS, AND CHILI

Wish I had time for one more bowl of chili.
Alleged dying words of Kit Carson

There is nothing so satisfying as a flavorful soup to start a meal or a hearty bowl of chili to make a meal. With a rich flavorful stock or zesty combinations of chilies and vegetables, soup can be as filling as it is nourishing. Chilled Gazpacho on a warm summer day made with fresh ripe tomatoes, crisp cucumbers, sweet bell peppers, and fresh cilantro or a tantalizing bowl of Turkey Chili or Tortilla Soup topped with crisp tortilla strips can fit right into today's healthy lifestyle. The soups in this book are all low in fat and most of them will freeze well. All soups and chilies are best when made a day in advance, allowing the flavors to develop—good news for busy cooks!

◀ *Black Bean Turkey Chili with Corn Muffins* (Recipe on page 88)

TORTILLA SOUP

Serves
8

Fat grams
14

Calories
295

Tortilla Soup can be a meal in itself. You may use chicken, smoked turkey, or simply serve the soup with cheese, tortilla strips, and avocado. Cooking the chicken in the soup stock gives both the stock and the chicken good flavor, but if you have leftover smoked turkey or chicken, this is a good way to use the leftovers.

2	white onions, quartered
5	tomatoes, unpeeled, cores intact
	Vegetable oil
4	cloves garlic, chopped
2	14 1/2-ounce cans chicken broth
3	cups water
6	chicken breasts, bone in, fat and skin removed
1	ancho chili pod, stemmed, seeded, and toasted
1	tablespoon vegetable oil
1	teaspoon ground cumin
2	corn tortillas, cut in small pieces
1/2	teaspoon coarse ground black pepper
1	teaspoon salt
	Pinch cayenne pepper
1	tablespoon fresh cilantro, minced
1-2	tablespoons fresh basil, minced

Garnishes:

1	ripe (firm) avocado, cut in cubes
4	ounces low-fat cheddar cheese, grated
4	corn tortillas, in strips, toasted

Preheat an indoor or outdoor grill to the highest setting (or the middle oven rack to broil).

Rub onions and tomatoes with vegetable oil and grill on all sides until browned. Finish cooking in a 350° oven, on a cookie sheet, for about 15–20 minutes. Cut the tomatoes in quarters and transfer onions and tomatoes to a blender or food processor fitted with the metal blade, and blend with the chopped garlic. You may have to do this in several batches.

Put the blended tomatoes and onions in a large saucepan or stockpot. Add garlic, chicken broth, and water and bring to a boil. Add chicken breasts and ancho chili pod and return to a boil. Skim the foam from the top. Reduce the heat to low and simmer, uncovered, for 25 to 30 minutes. Remove chicken and cool. Bone and shred or cut the meat into small pieces.

In a small skillet, heat the oil and add cumin and tortillas. Stir and cook 1 to 2 minutes. Add the cumin and tortillas to the stock. Season the soup with pepper, salt, cayenne pepper, and fresh herbs.

Simmer the soup for 10 to 15 minutes to blend the flavors. Cool. Blend the soup in several batches in a blender or food processor fitted with the metal blade.

When ready to serve, bring the soup to a boil. Adjust salt and pepper to taste. Divide the chicken among eight soup bowls. Pour the hot broth on top and garnish each bowl with 3 or 4 pieces of avocado, grated cheese, and toasted tortilla strips.

CHICKEN LIME SOUP

This is a traditional Mexican soup that is very light and colorful.

*Makes
6–8 servings*

*Fat grams
8*

*Calories
215*

4	corn tortillas, in strips, toasted
2	chicken breasts, grilled, boned and cut in bite-sized pieces
3	stalks celery, chopped
1	onion, chopped
3	carrots, chopped
4	tablespoons white rice
3	14 1/2-ounce cans chicken broth
1/2	teaspoon garlic salt
1/4	teaspoon ground cloves
1/4	teaspoon thyme
1/2	teaspoon oregano
2	tablespoons fresh lime juice
2	Roma tomatoes, peeled and diced
1	avocado, peeled, pitted, diced
8	scallions, sliced
	Salt and pepper to taste
	Fresh lime wedges
	Sliced radishes

Prepare the tortilla strips and set aside for garnish. Season the chicken and moisten with 2 to 3 tablespoons chicken broth. Set aside.

Generously coat a 2-quart saucepan with a vegetable spray. Add celery, onion, and carrots and sauté 3 to 4 minutes or until softened. Add white rice, chicken broth, garlic salt, cloves, thyme, and oregano. Simmer, uncovered, for 20 to 30 minutes.

When you are ready to serve the soup, add the lime juice, tomatoes, avocado, scallions, and reserved chicken. Season to taste with salt and pepper.

Serve the soup with tortilla strips and fresh lime wedges.

Advance Preparation: The soup base may be prepared a day or two in advance. Add lime juice, tomatoes, avocado, and scallions before serving.

BLACK BEAN SOUP

Always a favorite, this soup is hearty enough to make a meal when served with a salad or soft tacos. Choose from any of the suggested garnishes or combine several for a colorful presentation. If you use Smoked Turkey Stock (p. 15), it will give the soup a rich, smoky flavor.

5	cups cooked Black Beans (p. 17)
1	14 1/2-ounce can chicken broth
1	4 1/2-ounce can green chilies
1	jalapeño chili, stemmed and seeded
1	8-ounce can tomato sauce
1–2	ounces dry sherry
1/2–1	teaspoon salt

Garnishes:

3	ounces grated Monterey Jack cheese
	Pico de Gallo (p. 24) or
	fresh diced tomatoes
	Poblano Cream (p. 37) or nonfat sour cream
	Sliced scallions, green and white part

Using a food processor fitted with the metal blade or a blender, blend the beans with 1/2 to 1 cup of the chicken broth, green chilies, jalapeño, and tomato sauce. You may have to do this in several batches.

Heat the blended beans with the remaining chicken broth and sherry in a large saucepan over medium heat, stirring occasionally, until hot. Season to taste with salt. Ladle into warm soup bowls. Serve the soup with bowls of garnish.

If using Poblano Cream or sour cream as a garnish, put it in a small zip-lock bag. Snip the corner with scissors and then drizzle cream on the hot soup.

Advanced Preparation: The soup may be prepared a day in advance. It may be necessary to add a little chicken stock when reheating.

*Makes about
7 cups
6 servings*

*Fat grams
8*

*Calories
470*

VEGGIE CHILI

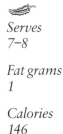

Serves
7–8

Fat grams
1

Calories
146

You can use black, pinto, or red beans. Roasting the bell peppers will enhance the flavor and is worth the extra time. Serve the chili with rice and cornbread muffins.

3	cloves garlic, minced
1	large red onion, chopped
1	cup chopped celery
1 1/2	cups chopped cauliflower
1	green bell pepper, chopped
1	red bell pepper, chopped
1 1/2	cups chopped carrots
2	cups chopped zucchini
1/4	cup chili powder
1	teaspoon ground cumin
1	14 1/2-ounce can vegetable broth
1 1/2	cups chopped mushroom
1	4 1/2-ounce can diced green chilies or
	2 poblano chilies, roasted, peeled, and diced
1	14 1/2-ounce can tomatoes, tomatoes chopped (including juices)
2–3	tablespoons yellow instant grits or cornmeal
1	tablespoon cider vinegar
	Salt and pepper to taste
1	cup pinto beans, including liquid

Garnish:

Sliced scallions
Low-fat grated cheese (optional)
Toasted tortilla strips

Coat a 3-quart saucepan with a vegetable spray. Add garlic, onion, and celery and sauté, stirring occasionally, until browned. Add cauliflower, bell pepper, carrots, and zucchini and cook, stirring to prevent burning, about 5 minutes. Add chili powder and cumin and stir to combine.

Add the beef broth, mushrooms, chilies, and tomatoes and cook, uncovered, for 20 minutes or until vegetables are tender and flavors are blended. Slowly add the cornmeal or grits, salt, pepper, and pinto beans, if using. Simmer about 5 to 8 minutes. If you prefer a thinner broth, reduce the amount of cornmeal or grits, or omit completely. Depending on the kind of chili powder used, you may need to add 1 tablespoon (or less) brown sugar.

Serve the chili in large soup bowls. Garnish with scallions, cheese, and tortilla strips.

Advance Preparation: Chili is best made a day in advance. Thin with broth if necessary.

GREEN CHILI
CHICKEN CHILI

Serves
8

Fat grams
11

Calories
390

This delicious chili may be made a day in advance and reheated. It makes a good "one-dish" meal when served with rice. The poblano chilies will make a spicier dish than canned green chilies.

4	cups cooked chicken
2	cloves garlic, minced
1	large onion, chopped
1	large zucchini, chopped
2	7-ounce cans mild green chilies or 5 poblano chilies, roasted and peeled
1	14 1/2-ounce can Mexican-style stewed tomatoes, tomatoes chopped
2	small potatoes, peeled and diced
1–2	cups chicken broth
1/2	teaspoon ground cumin
1	teaspoon oregano
1/2	teaspoons salt
	Coarse ground black pepper
1	package frozen corn, thawed
2	tablespoons fresh cilantro

Garnish:

Crema (p. 21)
Shredded lettuce
Thinly sliced radishes

Shred or dice the chicken and set aside.

Heat a large saucepan over medium heat and coat generously with a vegetable spray. Add the garlic and onion, and sauté 2 to 3 minutes. Stir in zucchini and continue cooking until zucchini is softened. Add chilies, tomatoes, potatoes, chicken broth, cumin, and oregano and simmer, uncovered, for 15 minutes or until vegetables are very tender.

Add salt, pepper, corn, and reserved chicken. Return to a simmer and simmer just long enough to heat through. Stir in cilantro.

Serve the chili in large bowls with assorted garnishes.

SHRIMP GAZPACHO

This is just as good without the shrimp (and lower in calories). It's almost "free" from fat, very low in calories, and full of flavor.

Serves 6

Fat grams 1.5

Calories 138

1/2	sweet Texas onion, cut in 6 pieces
2	cloves garlic, sliced
4	ripe tomatoes, peeled, cored, and quartered
2	small cucumbers, peeled and cut in chunks
1	red bell pepper, diced
2	serrano chilies, stemmed, seeded
1/4	cup red wine vinegar
4	cups tomato or tomato/vegetable juice
2	tablespoons tomato paste
2	sprigs each parsley and basil
1/2	teaspoon salt
1/2	cup diced green bell pepper
1/2	cup diced red bell pepper (reserved)
1/2	cup diced cucumber (reserved)
1/2	pound cooked shrimp, chopped coarsely
6	lime wedges
	Thin tortilla strips, toasted

If Texas sweet onions are not available, use a sweet red onion. Cut in 6 pieces and soak in ice water 15 minutes before blending.

Using a blender or food processor fitted with the metal blade, blend the garlic, tomatoes, and onion. Set aside 1/2 cup each diced red bell pepper and diced cucumber. Blend the remaining cucumber and peppers along with serrano chilies and vinegar. Add 1 cup of the tomato juice, tomato paste, parsley, basil, and salt. (You will have to do this in several batches.)

Combine the blended vegetables in a large bowl. Add remaining tomato juice and season with salt and pepper. Stir in reserved diced vegetables, green bell pepper, and chopped shrimp. Chill 2 hours before serving.

Serve each bowl with a lime wedge and toasted tortillas.

Advance Preparation: The soup may be prepared a day in advance. Add the shrimp before serving.

Roasted Corn and Grilled Vegetable Soup

Serves
8

Fat grams
2

Calories
123

The grilled vegetables add a rich flavor to this low-fat vegetable soup. Add cooked chicken or pinto beans to make a more substantial soup.

2	ears fresh corn, husks removed
1	large zucchini, sliced lengthwise in 4 strips
1	large yellow squash, sliced lengthwise in 4 strips
1	large onion, chopped
1	large turnip, peeled and diced
2	carrots, peeled and diced
2	14 1/2-ounce cans chicken or vegetable broth
1	16-ounce can Mexican-style stewed tomatoes, tomatoes chopped
1	green bell pepper, diced
1	red bell pepper, diced
1/2	teaspoon salt
1/4	teaspoon coarsely ground black pepper
1	tablespoon fresh minced cilantro
2	cups julienne spinach, uncooked
3	cups diced cooked chicken, optional
1	cup cooked pinto beans, optional

Garnish:

Toasted tortilla strips
Lime wedges

To cook the corn and squashes, heat the grill to the highest setting. Coat the vegetables with a vegetable spray and place them on the grill. Season with salt and pepper and grill on both sides until just tender. Cool and cut both squashes in 1/4-inch dice. Cut corn from the cob and set aside.

Place a large saucepan over medium heat. Coat generously with a vegetable spray and sauté the turnip, carrots, and onion, 3 to 4 minutes. Season with salt and pepper, turning often. Add about 1 cup of the chicken broth and bring to a boil. Simmer 3 to 5 minutes, then add remaining chicken broth and tomatoes.

Add bell peppers, corn, and squash and simmer until peppers are softened, about 5 to 6 minutes. Add salt, pepper, and cilantro to taste.

Add the spinach just prior to serving or place spinach in each serving bowl and pour the hot soup on top.

Serve with toasted tortillas and lime wedges.

If adding chicken, turkey, or beans, add them at the end with the salt and pepper and cook just long enough to heat.

BLACK BEAN
TURKEY CHILI

An answer to leftover turkey, this chili makes a good buffet dish for your winter football get-togethers. You may use green chilies in place of poblano chilies; however, the flavor and color of poblano chilies are superior.

*Serves
10*

*Fat grams
4–6*

*Calories
250–275*

1	tablespoon safflower oil
1	red onion, diced
1	white onion, diced
4	cloves garlic, minced
4	poblano chilies, roasted, peeled, and diced
1	red bell pepper, roasted, peeled, and diced
2	cups green bell pepper, diced
1/3	cup chili powder
1	teaspoon ground cumin
7–8	cups chicken broth
2	pounds turkey meat, diced
1	cup corn kernels
1	cup cooked black beans, liquid drained
1/2–1	teaspoon salt
1/2	teaspoon black pepper
1	tablespoon cornmeal

Garnishes:

Green onions, sliced
Thinly sliced radishes
Nonfat sour cream
Low-fat cheese, grated

Heat the safflower oil over medium heat in a 6-quart saucepan. Add the onions and garlic and sauté until softened, about 5 minutes. Stir in the peppers, chilies, chili powder, and cumin.

Add the chicken broth and cook 25 to 30 minutes. Add turkey, corn, and black beans to the broth. Stir in salt, pepper, and cornmeal and simmer 10 to 15 minutes.

Serve with bowls of garnish and warm corn tortillas or corn muffins.

◀ *Grilled Swordfish with Tequila Lime Sauce and Confetti Beans* (Recipe on page 108)

CHILI CON CARNE

Serves
8

Fat grams
9 (without beans)
9.2 (with beans)

Calories
200 (without beans)
240 (with beans)

Fresh poblano chilies will add delicious flavor to the chili (no fat and minimal calories) and are well worth the trouble. You may substitute ground turkey for the beef with surprisingly good results. Venison is also a good choice if ground without added fat.

1 1/4	pound top round, coarsely ground
1	large onion, chopped
1	large green or red bell pepper, diced
6	tablespoons chili powder
1/2	teaspoon ground cumin
1	14 1/2-ounce can diced tomatoes, including juices, puréed or 2 8-ounce cans tomato sauce
2	tablespoons cornmeal
1	fresh poblano chili, roasted, peeled and diced, optional
2	14 1/2-ounce cans beef broth
1	tablespoon apple cider vinegar
1/2	teaspoon oregano
1/2–1	teaspoon salt
	Fresh cracked black pepper
1	14 1/2-ounce can pinto beans, undrained

Garnishes:

1	bunch scallions, sliced
	Low-fat grated cheese

Place a 4-quart saucepan over medium high heat. Add the beef and sear, without stirring, until browned. Break up the meat with a fork and cook 3 to 4 minutes, stirring until juices no longer run pink. Place the meat in a strainer and press to strain the juices in a small bowl. Place the bowl in the freezer to solidify fat for easy removal. Return the meat to the same pan, add onion and bell pepper, and continue cooking over medium-high heat. Stir in chili powder and cumin, then add tomatoes or tomato sauce and cornmeal. Continue to stir, adding poblano chili, if using, and remaining ingredients except salt and pepper. Simmer the chili over medium-low heat for 30 minutes, stirring occasionally.

Remove the bowl from the freezer. Remove and discard the solid fat from the top. Add the broth to the chili. Season the chili with salt and pepper. If using beans, add them last. Heat thoroughly and adjust salt and pepper to taste.

Serve the chili with bowls of sliced scallions and low-fat grated cheese.

PINTO BEAN SOUP

Pinto beans and roasted peppers make a delicious, hearty soup.

Serves 6

Fat grams
1

Calories
184

1	green bell pepper, roasted, peeled, diced
1	yellow bell pepper, roasted, peeled, diced
2	poblano chilies, roasted, peeled, diced
2	ounces smoked turkey, diced fine
1	large onion, chopped
2	cloves garlic, minced
1	14 1/2-ounce can beef broth
1/2	teaspoon cumin
1/2	teaspoon chili powder
1	14 1/2 ounce-can Mexican-style tomatoes, tomatoes chopped
3	cups cooked pinto beans including liquid
	Salt and pepper to taste
2	tablespoons fresh cilantro

Roast bell peppers and place them in a covered bowl. Peel peppers over the bowl so all the flavorful juices may be reserved. Discard all seeds, stems, and peel. (It is not necessary to save poblano chili juices.)

Place a 2-quart saucepan over medium heat. Coat generously with a vegetable spray. Add the turkey and onion and sauté, stirring constantly until lightly browned, about 4 to 5 minutes. Add garlic, 1/2 cup beef broth, cumin, and chili powder. Bring to a boil and add remaining beef broth, tomatoes, pinto beans, diced peppers, and chilies. Simmer 8 to 10 minutes.

Season with salt, pepper, and fresh cilantro.

MAIN DISHES

*The discovery of a new dish does more for the happiness
of man than the discovery of a star.*

Brillat-Savarin, French gastronome

Where or when the first platter of sizzling fajitas started is a topic for heated discussion, but one thing everyone agrees on is that their instant popularity spread like wild fire. Freshly grilled meats, chicken, pan-seared onions and peppers with warm, soft tortillas, pico de gallo, and guacamole have universal appeal. When prepared at home, fajitas can be a light, healthy meal.

Light entrées in this section are not limited to fajitas. Red Snapper Veracruz, a classic Mexican dish, makes cooking fish as easy as it is light. Other seafood entrées are grilled or oven roasted and rely on assertive marinades, warm salsas, light vinaigrettes, or a spicy glaze for added flavor and zest.

Chicken Margarita is marinated in tequila and lime, which both tenderizes and flavors. Halibut is oven roasted with spicy chili pesto and fresh, sweet tomatoes. Skinless chicken breast is crusted with cornbread crumbs and a sprinkling of pecans to make an entrée that defies its low fat grams.

Some advance preparation is possible in all the main dishes, making them suitable for entertaining. Seafood and shellfish are emphasized to keep the main entrée on the lighter side and to save some room for appetizers and desserts!

◀ *Cornbread Crusted Chicken with Red Bell Pepper Sauce* (Recipe on page 118)

FAJITAS

The popularity of this dish is due in no small measure to the "sizzling" presentation popularized by restaurants. Fajitas are no longer limited to beef and chicken. Pork, shrimp, catfish, vegetables—even apple pie—are served on sizzling platters.

The marinade that follows can be used for beef, chicken, and fish. The Sizzling Sauce is great for reheating fajitas. The good thing about fajitas is you can make all the accompaniments in advance and have everything done before your guests arrive. Be aware of the amount of sour cream, cheese, and guacamole you add to each tortilla—that's where the fat and calories add up.

If you serve fajitas with onions and peppers, put both on the sizzling platter, side by side.

For all fajitas, fat grams and calories are for meat, poultry, shrimp, or vegetables only. Add fat grams and calories for each corn or flour tortilla as well as the accompaniments (see p.3).

The Marinade:

6	cloves garlic, minced
1/3	cup fresh lime juice
2	jalapeño chilies, chopped
3	tablespoons Worcestershire sauce
1/2	cup chopped onion
1/2	cup white wine
1/2	tablespoon coarse ground black pepper
2	cups safflower oil

The Accompaniments:

1	head thinly sliced Romaine lettuce
	Skinny Guacamole (p. 39)
	Pico de Gallo (p. 24)
1	cup light sour cream
8	ounces low-fat cheddar cheese, grated
	Grilled Onions and Peppers (recipe follows)

Sizzling Sauce:

1/2	cup chicken or beef broth
3	tablespoons soy sauce
2	tablespoons light butter, melted
1/4	cup white wine

Fresh lime wedges
6 corn or flour tortillas or
   warmed pita halves

Fat grams
1 per tablespoon

Calories
12 per tablespoon

Beef Fajitas

2 1/2	pounds top round or flank steak
	Salt and pepper

Serves
6

Fat grams
17 (flank)
10 (round)

Calories
360 (flank)
300 (round)

Trim the meat of all visible fat. Lightly pound with a meat tenderizer to an even thickness. Marinate 3 to 4 hours, covered and refrigerated.

Heat an outdoor grill to make a hot fire. Remove the meat from the marinade and season with salt and pepper. Grill on both sides over the hot fire about 2 minutes per side. Cover and set aside.

Heat the sizzling sauce in a small pan. Cut the meat into thin strips. Place an iron skillet over high heat. Add a few drops of oil and stir-fry the meat a few seconds to reheat. Drizzle with the sizzling sauce, and serve with warm flour tortillas and accompaniments. Makes enough for two per person.

The Onions and Peppers

1	onion, in julienne strips
1	red bell pepper, in julienne strips
1	yellow bell pepper, in julienne strips
1	green bell pepper, in julienne strips
	Salt and pepper

Serves
4

Fat grams
1

Calories
40

Place a large skillet over medium heat. Coat with a vegetable spray. Add the onions and peppers and stir-fry until lightly browned. Season with salt and pepper. Drizzle with the sizzling sauce and serve with beef, chicken, or shrimp fajitas.

Chicken Fajitas

Serves
8

Fat grams
5

Calories
190 (chicken only)

8   **large, skinless chicken breast filets**
       Salt and pepper

Trim visible fat from the chicken and lightly pound to an even thickness with a meat tenderizer. Marinate 2–3 hours, refrigerated.

Season the chicken with salt and pepper and grill over a hot fire about 1 1/2 minutes per side. Remove, cover, and set aside.

Heat the sizzling sauce in a small pan. Cut the chicken into thin strips. Place an iron skillet over high heat. Add a few drops of oil and stir-fry the chicken strips a few seconds to reheat. Drizzle with the sizzling sauce and serve with warm flour tortillas and accompaniments. Makes enough for 2 per person.

Shrimp Fajitas

Serves
6

Fat grams
5

Calories
181 (shrimp only)

2   **tablespoons fresh cilantro**
2   **pounds large shrimp (21–25 count)**
       Salt and pepper

Stir the fresh cilantro into the marinade. Peel and devein the shrimp and remove tails. Marinate 30 minutes. Skewer large shrimp on wooden skewers and grill over a hot fire about 1 minute per side. Cool, then halve the shrimp by cutting through the back to make thin slices.

Heat the sizzling sauce in a small pan. Place an iron skillet over medium heat. Add a few drops of oil and stir-fry the shrimp a few seconds to reheat. Drizzle with the sizzling sauce and serve with warm flour tortillas and accompaniments. Makes enough for 2 per person.

Vegetable Fajitas

2	carrots, diagonally sliced
2	yellow squash, diagonally sliced
2	zucchini, diagonally sliced
10	large mushrooms, halved
1	red bell pepper, in wide strips
1	yellow bell pepper, in wide strips
1	green bell pepper, in wide strips
1	bunch scallion, white part only
12	cherry tomatoes

*Serves
4*

*Fat grams
1*

*Calories
100 (vegetables
only)*

Blanch the carrots in boiling salted water for 1 minute.

It is not necessary to marinate the vegetables; simply brush with olive or safflower oil and season with salt and pepper. Grill over a hot fire until well marked and just tender. Cut the squashes into strips.

Place the vegetables on a heated iron skillet and drizzle with a small amount of the sizzling sauce. Serve with accompaniments and fresh lime wedges.

Swordfish or Tuna Fajitas

2	tablespoons fresh minced cilantro
4	6–ounces swordfish or tuna steaks
	Salt and pepper
	Sizzling Sauce (p. 101)

Serves 6

*Fat grams
6*

*Calories
210*

(Swordfish only)

Stir the fresh cilantro into the marinade. Marinate the fish for about 30 mintues. Heat an outdoor grill to make a hot fire. Remove the fish and grill about 2–3 minutes per side. Season with salt and pepper.

Heat the sizzling sauce. Cut the fish in thin strips. Place an iron or nonstick skillet over medium heat. Add a few drops of oil and stir-fry the strips a few seconds to reheat. Drizzle with the Sizzling Sauce and serve as directed above. Makes enough for 2 per person.

Red Snapper Veracruz

....

Serves
6

Fat grams
10

Calories
453

Almost any flaky white fish may be used for this dish. Choose from halibut, grouper, flounder, or redfish. This is a good dish for entertaining and a foolproof way to cook fish at home. Serve the snapper with Mexican Rice and grilled vegetables or a simple salad with shredded lettuce, diced tomatoes, and toasted tortilla strips.

6	8-ounce fish filets
2	fresh limes
	Juice from 1/2 orange

The Sauce:

1	tablespoon safflower oil
2	cloves garlic, minced
1	red onion, in short julienne strips
1/2	green bell pepper, in short julienne strips
1	14 1/2-ounce can Mexican-style stewed tomatoes
2	large poblano chilies, roasted, peeled, cut in short julienne strips
1	tablespoon red wine vinegar
10	pitted black olives, sliced
3	tablespoons capers
1	8-ounce can tomato sauce
1/2–1	teaspoon salt
1/4	teaspoon coarsely ground black pepper
1	tablespoon minced cilantro

Garnish:

A small bowl of pickled jalapeño chilies
Minced fresh parsley

Preheat the oven to 375°.

Place the filets in a 9 × 13 baking dish and season with salt and pepper. Squeeze the juice from the limes and orange over the filets.

Heat the oil in a large skillet over medium heat and sauté the garlic, onion, and bell pepper until translucent. Add the stewed tomatoes and poblano chilies and bring the sauce to a simmer. Stir in the remaining ingredients and remove from the heat.

Spoon the sauce over the fish and bake, uncovered, at 375° for 8 minutes. Cover loosely with foil and bake an additional 4 to 6 minutes. Remove the fish with a spatula to heated serving plates. Transfer the sauce to a saucepan and bring to a boil, stirring constantly.

Spoon the sauce on each filet and garnish with fresh minced parsley. Serve pickled jalapeños on the side.

Advance Preparation: The sauce may be made a day in advance and reheated.

Grilled Red Snapper with Warm Shrimp Salsa

Serves
6

Fat grams
10

Calories
453

I've also prepared this recipe with fresh lump crabmeat, when in season, with excellent results. The ingredients and methods are the same; however, the crab requires less cooking time because it is already cooked.

6	8-ounce red snapper filets
	Safflower or olive oil
	Salt and pepper

Warm Shrimp Salsa:

1	tablespoon light butter
1	tablespoon safflower oil
2	shallots, minced
1	clove garlic, minced
1 1/2	cups coarsely chopped shrimp, peeled, deveined
1/4	cup rice wine vinegar
	Juice from 1/2 lemon
2	serrano chilies, stemmed, seeded, diced
1	cup peeled, diced tomatoes
1	small avocado, diced
1/2	cup diced mango (ripe but firm)
1	tablespoon fresh cilantro
	Salt and pepper

Preheat the grill to make a hot fire.

Coat the filets with oil on both sides and season with salt and pepper. Rub the grill with an oil-dampened rag to prevent the fish from sticking. Grill the filets on one side about 5 minutes.

Using a spatula, carefully turn the fish and grill on the opposite side about 3 minutes. Allow 7 to 8 minutes per 1-inch thickness of fish. Remove the filets to a plate, cover, and keep warm while preparing the salsa.

Heat the butter and oil in a medium skillet over medium heat. Add the shallots, garlic, and shrimp. Sauté 2 to 3 minutes or until the shrimp turns pink.

Add the vinegar, lemon juice, chilies, and tomatoes. Cook just long enough to heat the tomatoes and combine ingredients. Remove from heat and gently stir in avocado and cilantro. Season with salt and pepper.

Spoon the warm salsa over grilled fish and garnish with several sprigs of fresh cilantro.

GRILLED
SWORDFISH WITH
TEQUILA LIME
VINAIGRETTE

....

Serves
6

Fat grams
34

Calories
600

Grilled swordfish or tuna may be served with any of the salsas in this book. This simple reduction of citrus and tequila makes the base for a "salsa" vinaigrette that is both colorful and delicious with grilled fish.

Basting Sauce:

2	garlic cloves
2	shallots
3	serrano chilies
1/2	cup cilantro sprigs
3/4	cup safflower or olive oil
1/2	teaspoon coarse salt

Tequila Lime Vinaigrette:

1/3	cup tequila
2	tablespoons triple sec
1/4	cup fresh lemon juice
1/4	cup fresh lime juice
1	shallot, minced
1	garlic clove, minced
2	tablespoons rice wine vinegar
2	tablespoons safflower oil
1/3	cup finely diced mango
1/3	cup finely diced red bell pepper, roasted, and peeled
1/2	tablespoon fresh basil, minced
1/2	tablespoon fresh cilantro, minced
	Salt and pepper to taste

| 6 | 8-ounce swordfish steaks |
| | Salt and pepper |

Garnish:

Fresh basil sprig

Prepare a gas or charcoal grill and preheat to make a hot fire.

In a blender combine the garlic, shallots, serrano chilies, and cilantro. Blend on high speed. Add the oil and salt and set aside.

To make the vinaigrette, put tequila, triple sec, lemon juice, lime juice, shallot, garlic, and vinegar in a small pan over high heat. Bring to a boil and reduce the liquid by half of the original volume. Remove from the heat and whisk in the oil. Add the mango, red bell pepper, and fresh herbs. Season with salt, pepper, basil, and cilantro.

Trim dark meat from the swordfish and remove skin. Put the swordfish on a platter and brush both sides with the basting sauce.

Place the fish on the grill, season with salt and pepper, and grill 5 minutes. Turn and grill on the opposite side and cook about 3 minutes. Allow about 7 to 8 minutes total time per 1-inch thickness of the fish.

Ladle the sauce on top of each filet. Garnish with fresh basil.

Pepper Glazed Salmon

....

Serves
6

Fat grams
18

Calories
498

The sweet-hot sauce compliments both the salmon and the fresh pineapple salsa. Serve this with spoon bread or a selection of grilled vegetables.

6	8-ounce salmon filets
	Salt and pepper
2	tablespoons light butter
1	cup jalapeño jelly
1	tablespoon white wine vinegar
	Pineapple-Pepper Salsa (p. 32)

Preheat the oven to broil.

Cover a baking pan with foil and coat with a vegetable or olive oil spray. Season the salmon filets with salt and pepper and place on the foil.

In a small skillet, melt the butter and drizzle over the fish. In the same pan, melt the jelly with the vinegar over low heat. The jelly need not be fully melted. Spoon over the fish.

Broil, uncovered, 6 inches from the heating element for 6 to 8 minutes or until lightly browned. Turn the oven to 350°, cover the pan with foil, and bake 4 to 5 minutes or until fish flakes easily with a fork.

Serve each filet with Pineapple Salsa.

Pesto Roasted Halibut with Yellow Bell Pepper Sauce (Recipe on page 112) ▶

PESTO ROASTED HALIBUT

Serves
4

Fat grams
12

Calories
491

This combination of textures and flavors gives a mild fish a new personality. While the pesto is spicy by itself, the combination is not *hot*—just flavorful. The Roasted Pepper Sauce may be made with red or yellow bell peppers and compliments both the pesto and the fish. You may also use swordfish, red snapper, orange roughy, or flounder.

Yellow Bell Pepper Sauce:

2	large yellow bell peppers, roasted and peeled
1	large shallot, minced
2	cloves garlic, minced
1/4	cup white wine
	Juice from 1/2 lemon
1/2	cup chicken broth
1	tablespoon cornstarch
1 1/2	ounces fat-free cream cheese
	Salt and pepper
4	8-ounce halibut filets
	Salt and pepper
	Spicy Green Chili Pesto (p. 20)
2	tablespoons light butter, melted
1	cup diced tomatoes

Garnish:

Fresh cilantro
Thin tortilla strips

Preheat the oven to 400°.

To make the sauce, cut the peppers into small pieces and place in a blender jar. Add all accumulated juices from the peppers. Blend to chop.

In a small saucepan heat the shallot and garlic in white wine over medium heat for a few minutes or until garlic is softened. Add to the blender jar and blend with the peppers until smooth. Add chicken broth, cornstarch, and cream cheese and blend on high to mix well. Pour the blended mixture into a small saucepan over medium heat and stir constantly for 3 to 4 minutes or until the sauce is thickened and hot. Season with salt and pepper. If the sauce is not completely smooth, blend again.

Coat the fish with an olive oil spray and season with salt and pepper. Place filets in a roasting pan, and add 1 cup each white wine and water. The filets should not be submerged in the liquid. Spread about 1 tablespoon pesto over each filet and drizzle with butter. Roast for 5 minutes, then top each filet with diced tomatoes and cook an additional 5 to 8 minutes or until fish flakes easily with a fork.

Ladle one-fourth the sauce onto each serving plate, covering one half the plate. Place the halibut in the center.

Garnish with fresh cilantro and thin tortilla strips.

Advance Preparation: Both the sauce and the pesto may be made a day in advance.

Arroz Marisco

··

Serves
8

Fat grams
9

Calories
412

This combination of rice and shellfish is a perfect "one-dish" meal for entertaining. Serve it with a Caesar Salad, fresh hot cornbread, and black beans. Use any combination of fresh shellfish or use all shrimp or lobster.

2	cloves garlic, minced
1	onion, diced
1	red bell pepper, diced
1	yellow bell pepper, diced
3	fresh jalapeño chilies, minced
1	tablespoon safflower oil
2	teaspoons chili powder
1/2	cup white wine
1 1/2	cups long grain white rice
1	14 1/2-ounce can chicken broth
1	cup water
2	tablespoons lemon juice
1	cup chopped canned tomatoes, juices drained
1	package frozen peas, thawed
1 1/2	pounds assorted fresh shellfish (shrimp, scallops and lobster) cleaned, deveined, and cut in small pieces
1–2	tablespoons fresh parsley or cilantro
	Salt and pepper to taste

Coat a 3-quart saucepan with a vegetable spray. Add the garlic, onion, and peppers and sauté over medium heat 2 to 3 minutes or until vegetables are softened.

Add the safflower oil and chili powder and stir to combine.

Add the white wine, rice, chicken broth, water, and lemon juice and bring to a boil. Cover and simmer over medium-low heat for 18 minutes.

Remove the cover and add tomatoes, peas, and shellfish. Gently stir a few times to combine. Cover again and continue to cook over low heat for 8 minutes. Remove from heat and let stand for 5 minutes. Add additional liquid if necessary.

Season with fresh cilantro or parsley, salt, and pepper.

Note: If using cooked shellfish, reduce the cooking time by 6 minutes.

GRILLED SALMON

Freshly grilled salmon needs only a little oil and lemon because a preheated, hot grill seals in the natural juices.

Serves
6

Fat grams
12 (with sauce)

Calories
508 (with sauce)

Spicy Tartar Sauce:

2	cloves garlic
1	2–3 inch piece celery
1	2–3 inch piece cucumber, seeded
6	springs fresh cilantro
4	ounces fat-free cream cheese
4	tablespoons light mayonnaise
1/2	teaspoon fresh lemon juice
4	scallions, sliced (green and white part)
1	tablespoon pimento, juices drained
1	tablespoon capers
2	hard boiled egg whites, diced
2	tablespoons pickled jalapeño chilies
	Salt and pepper
1	4–5 pound salmon, filleted or 6 salmon filets, about 8 ounces each
	Olive oil
	Salt and pepper juice from 2 lemons

Garnish:

Lemon wedges

Put the garlic, celery, cucumber, and cilantro in a blender or food processor fitted with the metal blade and process to mince. Add cream cheese, mayonnaise, and lemon juice and blend again.

Stir in the scallions, pimento, capers, egg white, and jalapeño chilies by hand. Season to taste with salt and pepper.

Preheat a gas or charcoal grill to make a hot fire. Rub the salmon with olive and season with salt and pepper. Dampen a cloth with oil and using tongs, wipe the grill surface. Place the rack about 5 to 6 inches from the heat.

Place filets on the grill, brush with lemon juice, and cook until the edges begin to turn opaque, about 4 to 5 minutes. Using a spatula, carefully turn the fish and grill on the opposite side 3 to 4 minutes. Brush again with oil and lemon juice.

Serve the salmon with Spicy Tartar Sauce, fresh lemon wedges, and grilled vegetables.

CHICKEN MARGARITA

....

Serves
4

Fat grams
5

Calories
500

The chicken preparation is a little trouble but makes an attractive presentation for a special occasion. If you prefer, you can use grilled chicken breasts. Either way, this is a fun and flavorful Southwestern dinner.

The Marinade:

3	cloves garlic, minced
1/2	cup fresh lime juice
1/2	cup tequila
2	tablespoons sugar
1	teaspoon coarse salt
1	cup safflower or olive oil
1/2	tablespoon coarse ground black pepper
1	teaspoon crushed chili flakes

4	large single chicken breasts, wing tip attached
2–3	tablespoons fresh parsley
1/2	cup chicken broth

Black Bean Sauce:

Makes
5 cups

Fat grams
trace

Calories
20 per tablespoon

1	tablespoon minced garlic
2	tablespoon minced shallots
1/4	cup white wine
1/8	cup sherry
1 1/2	cups cooked black beans
2-3	cups chicken broth
1	teaspoon chili powder
1	tablespoon minced cilantro
	Salt and pepper to taste

Garnishes:

	Pico de Gallo (p. 24) or
	Mango Salsa (p. 31)
1/2	recipe Green Chili Spoon Bread (p. 170)

Preheat the oven to 400°.

Combine the marinade ingredients and place in a 7 × 11 glass dish.

Remove skin and visible fat from the chicken breasts. Using a sharp knife, remove the breast bones and cut the joint at the wing to release the wing. Clip the wing end, leaving only the meatier joint. Trim away the skin and flesh from the end of the wing. Place chicken breasts in the marinade and refrigerate 2 hours.

Prepare the black bean sauce. Heat a 2-quart saucepan over medium heat. Coat with a vegetable spray and add garlic and shallots. Stirring constantly, sauté 1 to 2 minutes, then add white wine, sherry, black beans, and 1 1/2 cup chicken broth. Bring to a simmer and cook 6 to 8 minutes, stirring frequently. Transfer the beans to a blender or food processor fitted with the metal blade and blend until very smooth.

Pour the puréed beans back into the same pan over medium-low heat. Add chili powder and enough additional chicken broth to make a sauce the consistency of heavy cream. Season with cilantro, salt, and pepper.

Remove the chicken from the marinade. Take the narrow end of the breast and pull it around to the base of the wing joint. Secure with a toothpick. Place the breasts in a baking dish just large enough to accommodate all four breasts.

Season with salt and pepper. Using a pastry brush, brush the flesh with the marinade and sprinkle with minced parsley. Pour 1/2 cup of the marinade in the pan along with 1/2 cup chicken broth.

Bake the chicken on the middle rack, at 400°, 15 minutes. Turn the setting to broil for about 5 minutes, until top is lightly browned.

Pool half of each serving plate with Black Bean Sauce. Remove toothpicks and place the chicken on the sauce. Serve the spoon bread in a tamale husk and garnish the plates with Pico de Gallo and fresh cilantro.

Advance Preparation: The marinade, Black Bean Sauce, and salsa may be made 1 day in advance.

CORNBREAD CRUSTED CHICKEN

*Serves
5*

*Fat grams
20*

*Calories
495*

This is a good way to bake skinless chicken breasts to preserve the natural juices. Try the same recipe for fish filets such as catfish, halibut, or red snapper as both the cornbread crust and Roasted Red Pepper Sauce will compliment fish as well as chicken. See the baking instruction for cooking time at the end of the recipe. The fat grams and calories include the sauce.

Roasted Red Pepper Sauce:

2	large red bell peppers, roasted and peeled
2	cloves garlic, minced
2	shallots, minced
1/4	cup white wine
	Juice from 1 lemon
1/2	cup chicken broth
1	tablespoon cornstarch
1 1/2	ounces fat-free cream cheese
1	tablespoon tomato paste
	Salt and pepper

The Cornbread Topping:

1 1/2	cups cornbread crumbs (about 8 mini muffins)
2	tablespoons finely diced pecans
1/4	teaspoon cayenne pepper
2	tablespoons fresh minced parsley
10	chicken breasts, skinless, boneless
	Salt and pepper
1/2	cup chicken broth
3	tablespoons light butter
1	cup chicken broth
1/2	cup white wine
	Juice from 1/2 lemon

Preheat the oven to broil. Place the rack in the middle of the oven.

To make the sauce, cut the peppers in small pieces and place in a blender. Turn the blender on/off to chop. Coat a small skillet with a vegetable spray and sauté the garlic and shallots a few minutes to soften, then add white wine and lemon. Blend with peppers until smooth. Add chicken broth and cornstarch and blend again.

Transfer to a small saucepan and cook over medium heat until thickened, about 2 to 3 minutes. Stir in cream cheese and tomato paste. Season to taste with salt and pepper. If the sauce is not smooth, blend again.

Combine the cornbread crumbs with pecans. Sprinkle cayenne pepper and parsley over the top and toss with two forks to disperse seasoning evenly.

Coat a baking dish with a vegetable spray. Season chicken with salt and pepper on both sides and place in the dish. Put about 1 1/2 tablespoons of the topping on each one. Melt the butter in the chicken broth and moisten the crumb topping with about 2 teaspoons liquid. Position the rack in the center of the oven. Broil for 8 minutes or until lightly browned. Change the oven setting to bake and set the temperature at 350°. Pour the broth, wine, and lemon juice in the baking pan and bake an additional 6 to 7 minutes.

To serve, pool the plate with the sauce and serve two breasts per person. Garnish with sprigs of fresh parsley.

Cornbread Crusted Catfish: Position the baking pan one rack closer to the element. Broil for 5 minutes or until lightly browned, then change the setting to bake (350°) and cook an additional 3 to 4 minutes. Serve with Spicy Tartar Sauce (p. 115) or Grilled Corn Salsa (p. 25).

STUFFED CHILIES
POBLANO

Serves
6

Fat grams
18

Calories
322

The fillings and sauces for these flavorful chilies are limited only by your imagination. Poblano chilies are "hotter" than Anaheim chilies, so choose a filling that is mild.

6	large poblano chilies, roasted and peeled
	Picadillo (p. 124)

Tomato Sauce:

1	14 1/2-ounce can tomatoes, including juices
1–2	teaspoons safflower oil
3	tablespoons minced onion
1	clove garlic, finely minced
1	tablespoon fresh cilantro or basil, minced
	Salt and pepper to taste
1	cup light sour cream
1/4	cup chicken broth

Garnish:

2/3	cup sliced almonds or pumpkin seeds, toasted

Roast and peel the chilies, being careful not to tear the flesh. Use scissors to make a slit down the center and to cut away the seeds and membrane. Fill each chili with about 3/4 cup Picadillo and place in an 8-inch or 9-inch pie pan, with the stems towards the edge of the dish. Cover with foil and heat in a 375° oven for 10 to 15 minutes.

To make the sauce, purée the tomatoes in a blender or food processor fitted with the metal blade. Heat the oil in a medium skillet over medium heat and sauté garlic and onion until translucent, about 3 to 4 minutes. Add tomatoes and simmer 3 to 4 minutes stirring constantly. Season with fresh cilantro or basil, salt, and pepper.

Combine the sour cream and chicken broth. Season with salt and pepper. Place a dollop of cream on top of each baked chili. Pool each plate with tomato sauce and garnish with toasted almonds.

CHICKEN STUFFED CHILIES

Makes
6

Fat grams
22

Calories
438

This is one of my favorite combinations of flavors. Try serving the chilies with both the red and yellow bell pepper sauces for a colorful presentation.

The Filling:

4	chicken breasts, roasted
	Salt and pepper
2	shallots, minced
1	clove garlic, minced
2–3	tablespoons chicken broth
2	ounces low-fat goat cheese or low-fat ricotta cheese
2	ounces fat-free cream cheese
6	large poblano chilies, roasted and peeled (stems intact)

Yellow Bell Pepper Sauce (p. 112)
Roasted Red Bell Pepper Sauce (p. 118)

1	cup cornbread crumbs (about 6 miniature muffins)
3	tablespoons chopped pecans
1	tablespoon minced cilantro
1/4	cup chicken broth
2	tablespoons light butter, melted

Garnish:

Fresh cilantro sprigs

Cook the chicken as directed and shred or cut the meat into small pieces. Season with salt and pepper.

Coat a medium skillet with vegetable spray and sauté garlic and shallots over medium heat until softened. Add chicken broth, cream cheese, and goat or ricotta cheese and remove from heat. Stir to combine the cheeses. Season with salt and pepper. Fold cheese mixture into the chicken.

Using scissors, make a slit on the side of each chili and remove seeds and veins carefully. Stuff each chili with the chicken and cheese mixture. Spray an 8-inch or 9-inch round pie pan with a vegetable oil and place chilies in a circle, stems overlapping the dish.

Preheat the oven to 375°.

Prepare the bell pepper sauces and set aside. Combine the cornbread crumbs with pecans and cilantro. Melt the butter in the chicken broth.

Top each chili with 1 to 2 tablespoons cornbread crumbs. Moisten the crumbs with butter and chicken broth. Put remaining crumbs on a cookie sheet, moisten with broth, and bake with the chilies. Cover the chilies with foil and bake for 8 minutes. Uncover and bake 12 to 15 minutes or until heated through and the crumbs are lightly browned. Toast additional crumbs at the same time until lightly browned.

For individual servings, pool each plate with the sauce and serve one chili per person. Sprinkle some of the toasted crumbs on the plate and garnish with fresh cilantro sprigs.

Advance Preparation: Sauce and chilies may be prepared a day in advance.

Other Suggested Fillings and Sauces:
1. Substitute shrimp for the chicken, add fresh corn kernels, and serve with Roasted Red Bell Pepper Sauce.
2. Fill chilies with Arroz Blanco (p. 168) and serve with a mild tomato sauce.

Chicken Stuffed Chilies with Red Bell Pepper Sauce and Yellow Bell Pepper Sauce (Recipes on pages 121, 112, and 118)▶

PICADILLO

....

Makes
4 1/2 to 5 cups

Fat grams
8

Calories
182 per 1/2 cup

Picadillo is a delicious filling for soft tacos, empanadas, spicy poblano chilies, or the Tamale Pie on page 163. While not exactly low-fat, duck is excellent in this recipe. For hunters of wild game, venison is a good choice, if ground without added fat.

1 1/4	pounds ground turkey
1	cup chopped onion
2	teaspoons chili powder
1/2	teaspoon ground cumin
1	smail apple, diced
1	4 1/2-ounce can diced green chilies
1	cup diced potato, skin on
1/2	14 1/2-ounce can Mexican-style stewed tomatoes, tomatoes chopped
1/2	cup beef broth
1	tablespoon apple cider vinegar
1/2	teaspoon ground cinnamon
1/4	teaspoon ground cloves
1/4	cup seedless raisins
1	teaspoon salt
	Pinch white pepper

Heat a large skillet over medium heat. Add the turkey and sear, without stirring, until browned. (Don't be concerned about the brown bits in the pan). When well browned, add the onion, chili powder, and cumin and mix in well, breaking up clumps of meat with a fork. Stir in the apple, chilies, potato, tomatoes, and beef broth. Simmer, covered 15 minutes.

Stir in the remaining ingredients and cook uncovered about 10 to 15 minutes or until vegetables are tender and most of the liquid has been absorbed. Adjust seasonings to taste.

For soft tacos, put a generous spoonful of Picadillo in a softened, warm flour or corn tortilla, fold over, and serve two per person. Garnish with one of the salsas or Pico de Gallo.

TAMALE PIE

Picadillo (p. 124)

The Topping:

3/4	cups yellow cornmeal
1/3	cup all purpose flour
2	teaspoons baking powder
1	tablespoon sugar
1/2	teaspoon salt
3	tablespoons light mayonnaise
1/2	cup skim milk
1/2	cup creamed corn
	Egg substitute equivalent to 1 egg

*Makes
8 servings*

*Fat grams
12*

*Calories
313*

Preheat the oven to 375°.

Put the Picadillo in a 10-inch, deep-dish pie pan. To make the topping, combine the dry ingredients in a mixing bowl. Stir in mayonnaise, milk, creamed corn, and egg. Spoon on top of the Picadillo and bake 20 minutes or until the topping tests done.

To serve, cut into wedges.

Advance Preparation: The Picadillo may be made two days in advance.

TORTILLA
SPECIALTIES

Let the quality of your ingredients speak to you. Taste things half done—and overdone. Taste everything you cook and take nothing for granted. Even your palate can change.

James Beard

Enchiladas, chalupas, tacos, tamale pie—these are the heart and soul of Mexican food. "Authentic" preparations of these wonderful foods often include massive amounts of lard or bacon fat to refry beans, to saturate corn tortillas to soften and seal them for enchiladas, to deep fry tortillas for tacos, chalupas, or chips, and to tenderize flour when making flour tortillas.

In this section, you'll find new techniques that bypass these fat-infused methods as well as enchilada sauces that range from fat-free to low-fat. Tomatillo Sauce, Ranchero Sauce, or Spicy Enchilada Sauce rely on combinations of tomatoes, chilies, onions, fresh herbs, and spices for their zesty flavors.

Enchilada and taco fillings range from chicken to combinations of cheese and vegetables. Chalupa shells topped with well-seasoned beans, grilled chicken, or fresh crabmeat with crisp lettuce, ripe tomatoes, and a fresh salsa are as easy to make as they are light.

When cooking all these Mexican favorites, always let your personal taste be your guide. Use the recipes to learn techniques for lighter, low-fat cooking and then adapt, adjust, or change to fit your lifestyle.

◀ *Cheese Enchiladas with Chili, Skinny Guacamole (left), and Arroz Blanco (right)*
(Recipes on pages 145, 39, and 168)

Tacos

*Fills 8 tacos or
8 enchiladas*

*Fat grams
Ground beef
(1/3 cup) 6.5
Ground turkey
(1/3 cup) 4*

*Calories
Beef (1/3 cup) 125
Turkey (1/3 cup) 95*

When testing this recipe with ground turkey, my "tasters" all thought the filling was beef. Using onions and adding green chilies add flavor and reduce the amount of meat (and calories) in each taco.

Taco Meat:

1	pound ground turkey or ground top round
1	cup diced yellow or white onion
1	clove garlic, minced
1 1/2	teaspoons chili powder
1	teaspoon oregano
1/2	cup tomato sauce
1/2	cup diced green chilies
1/2	teaspoon salt
1/4	teaspoon coarse ground black pepper

Heat a large skillet over medium heat. Add the turkey or ground round and sear over medium heat until browned, without stirring, about 5 to 6 minutes. (If using beef, pour off all rendered fat.) Add the onion, garlic, chili powder, and oregano and stir to break up clumps of meat. Sauté until the onion is fully cooked, about 3 to 4 minutes. Lower the heat to medium-low and stir in the tomato sauce and chilies.

Simmer until most of the liquid has evaporated, about 5 to 8 minutes. Add salt and pepper.

Beef Tacos (1)

*Fat grams
8*

*Calories
225*

Chicken Tacos(1)

*Fat grams
5*

*Calories
180*

To Make Tacos:

1. Prepare the taco shells by the toasting method on p. 2
2. For each taco, use:
   1/3 cup Taco Meat or Seasoned Chicken (p. 13)
   1/2 cup shredded iceberg and romaine lettuce
   1/2 ounce low-fat cheese, grated
   2 tablespoons fresh tomato, diced
   2 tablespoons picante sauce
3. Allow 2 to 3 tacos per person. Garnish plates with Crispy Greens (p. 8) and serve with pinto or Black Beans (p. 17)

GRILLED CHICKEN TACOS

*Makes
6*

*Fat grams
6 each*

*Calories
187 each*

Like most tacos, these make good snacks or a light meal. Poblano chilies will make spicier tacos, green chilies milder tacos. Or, for sensitive palates, use green bell peppers.

1/2	medium onion, in julienne strips
1/2	red bell pepper, in julienne strips
1/2	yellow bell pepper, in julienne strips
1/2	poblano chili, roasted, peeled, finely diced or 1/2 cup diced green chilies
2	grilled chicken breasts, thinly sliced
	Salt and pepper
6	flour tortillas or pita pockets, warmed
3	ounces low-fat mozzarella or Monterey Jack cheese, grated

Preheat the oven to 300°. Place a medium skillet over medium heat and coat generously with a vegetable spray. Sauté the onions and bell peppers, tossing constantly, until softened. You may need additional spray to keep the peppers from burning. Add chilies and chicken and toss together. Season with salt and pepper and cook long enough to heat the chicken.

Soften the tortillas if necessary in a microwave oven or non-stick skillet (p. 137). Divide the chicken mixture between six tortillas. Top each one with about 1/2 ounce cheese, then fold over and press down to seal.

Using a nonstick griddle or skillet, cook each tortilla quickly on both sides until lightly browned. Transfer each one to a cookie sheet and place in the oven while cooking the rest.

Serve with light sour cream and picante sauce.

VEGGIE TACOS

*Makes
8 pockets*

*Fat grams
4*

*Calories
114*

You may serve this colorful vegetable combination in pita pockets or flour tortillas. I've omitted cheese to make this low fat; however, a small amount of cheese or Mashed Black Beans (p. 19) in each taco makes a more substantial dish.

1	large carrot, thinly sliced diagonally
2	cups small broccoli florets
1	large zucchini squash
1	yellow squash
1	tablespoon vegetable oil
1	onion, julienne strips
2	cups sliced mushrooms
	Salt and pepper
2–3	tablespoons chicken or beef broth
1–2	teaspoons soy sauce
8	pita pockets or 8 flour tortillas
3	cups red tip leaf lettuce, thinly sliced
	Chunky Tomato Salsa (p. 28)

Bring 1 quart of salted water to a boil. Add carrot slices and cook 1 minute. Add broccoli florets and cook carrot and broccoli 1 minute together. Drain and refresh under cold water.

Halve zucchini and yellow squash lengthwise, and cut into slices.

Heat the vegetable oil in a large skillet over medium heat. Add the onion, squash, bell pepper, and mushrooms and season with salt and pepper. Sauté, tossing constantly, for 2 to 3 minutes. Add broccoli and carrot and cook 2 to 3 minutes or until vegetables are lightly browned and tender. Add chicken broth and soy sauce. Toss to coat and season vegetables.

Heat pita pockets or tortillas in a hot oven or microwave. Divide the vegetables between them. Fold tortillas over or roll like enchiladas. Serve 2 per person.

Garnish plates with lettuce and serve Chunky Salsa or picante sauce on the side.

Soft Chicken Tacos

These tacos, served like enchiladas, are served at La Fogata in San Antonio, one of my favorite restaurants. Jesse Calvillo, the owner, has a little of everything on his menu but was first among restaurant owners to offer some light alternatives. These tacos are equally good made with corn or flour tortillas, and are a good dish for the ladies when accompanied by Arroz Blanco (p. 168).

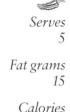

*Serves
5*

*Fat grams
15*

*Calories
454*

4	chicken breasts, bone in
	Salt and pepper
2–3	tablespoons chicken broth

The Sauce

1	clove garlic, minced
1 1/2	cup green bell pepper, in short strips or 1 cup diced green chilies
1	cup chopped onion
1	tablespoon safflower oil
2 1/2	cups chicken broth
2	ounces pimentos, drained
1/2	16-ounce can Mexican-style tomatoes, tomatoes chopped
2	tablespoons cornstarch
1/4–1/2	teaspoon salt
	Coarse ground black pepper

10	flour or corn tortillas
12	leaves Romaine lettuce, thinly sliced
3–4	ounces feta cheese, crumbled
2	corn tortillas, in thin strips, toasted (p. 2)
3/4	cup fresh diced tomatoes

Preheat the oven to 400°. Place the chicken in a roasting pan and season with salt and pepper. Roast for 30 minutes, then remove. When cool enough to handle, remove the skin and bone. Using two forks, shred the meat or cut into small pieces. Remove and discard all the fat. Season the chicken with salt and pepper and moisten with 2 to 3 tablespoons chicken broth.

To make the sauce, coat a 2-quart saucepan with a vegetable coating spray. Add garlic and onion and cook over medium heat about 1 minute. Add safflower oil and continue cooking, stirring constantly until onions are soft. Add chicken broth, tomatoes, and pimentos and bring to a boil. Dissolve the cornstarch in about 1/3 cup water. Stir to remove any lumps, then add it to the sauce. Cook, stirring constantly, until thickened, about 2 to 3 minutes. Season with salt and pepper.

Prepare and roll the tortillas with one of the methods on page 137.

Ladle the sauce across the center of the tortillas. Garnish with a handful of shredded lettuce, crumbled feta cheese, a few crisp tortilla strips, and diced tomatoes.

Advance Preparation: Both sauce and chicken may be prepared in advance.

Bean Chalupas

These are always popular as a snack, on a buffet table, or for a quick, light supper with a bowl of soup.

Makes
12 chalupas

Fat grams
3.5 each

Calories
154 each

12	corn tortillas
1	14 1/2-ounce can pinto beans, drained
1	cup diced onion
1/4	teaspoon chili powder
1/2	cup low-fat ricotta cheese
1/2	cup picante sauce
1/2	teaspoon garlic salt
	Salt and pepper to taste
2	cups red onion, julienne strips
3	cups Romaine lettuce, thinly sliced
2	cups iceberg lettuce, thinly sliced
4	ounces low-fat cheddar cheese, grated
1	cup diced tomatoes
6	large radishes, thinly sliced

Spray tortillas on both sides with a butter-flavored spray and sprinkle lightly with salt. Place directly on the rack and bake for 10 minutes at 350°. Remove and set aside.

Drain the pinto beans and discard liquid. Coat a medium skillet generously with a vegetable spray and cook the onion over medium heat, stirring constantly, until lightly browned. Put the onion in a food processor fitted with the metal blade and add the beans, chili powder, cheese, and picante sauce. Process to purée, then return to the same skillet, over medium heat. Add garlic salt, salt, and pepper to taste and heat until bubbling and hot. Set aside.

In a separate skillet, use a vegetable coating spray and sauté the red onion over medium heat, using vegetable spray, until browned, and set aside.

To assemble the chalupas, spread about 2 tablespoons of the beans on each tortilla. Top with combined lettuces, red onion, cheese, tomatoes, and radishes. Serve 2 or 3 per person.

Advance Preparation: You may prepare the beans a day in advance.

CHICKEN CHALUPAS

....

Makes
8

Fat grams
10.5 each

Calories
224 each

This is an attractive luncheon dish that you can prepare ahead and assemble prior to serving. For a more substantial meal, serve with Black Beans (p. 17) or Black Bean Soup (p. 87).

8	corn tortillas, toasted (p. 2)
4	large chicken breasts, bone in
1	cup picante sauce

Guacamole Dressing

1/4	cup diced green chilies
2	small tomatillos, skinned, rinsed, and quartered
1	clove garlic
4–5	sprigs fresh parsley or cilantro
1	avocado, peeled and cut in several pieces
4	tablespoons non-fat sour cream (or fat-free cream cheese)
1/2	teaspoon salt
	Pinch white pepper
8	tablespoons Mashed Beans (p. 19)
1	head Romaine lettuce, cut in strips

Garnish

2	ounces low-fat cheddar cheese, grated or 2 ounces crumbled feta cheese
1	cup diced tomatoes

Chicken Chalupas with Julienne Strip Jicama Salsa
(Recipes on pages 134 and 35). ▶

Preheat the oven to 400°. Season the chicken with your favorite seasoning salt, or salt and pepper, and roast for 30 to 35 minutes. Cool and remove skin and bones. Cut into small chunks and place in a small bowl. Toss with picante sauce and set aside.

To make the guacamole dressing, put the chilies, tomatillos, garlic, and parsley in a blender or food processor fitted with the metal blade and blend smooth. Add avocado and sour cream and blend again. Season with salt and pepper and refrigerate until ready to use.

To assemble the chalupas, place two crisp tortillas on each serving plate, overlapping. Spread each one with mashed beans. Place the lettuce on top of the beans, then mound the chicken on the lettuce. Spoon the guacamole on top, using about 1/4 cup per serving.

Garnish with grated cheese and diced tomatoes.

CRAB CHALUPAS

....

*Makes
12*

*Fat grams
3 each*

*Calories
154 each*

The combination of sweet, fresh crab and the spicy Poblano Cream makes a colorful, delicious, light chalupa.

1	pound fresh crabmeat
1	cup chopped red onion
1	cup fresh diced tomatoes
1/2	cup diced mango or papaya
2	tablespoons fresh cilantro
3-4	tablespoons fresh lemon juice
	Salt and pepper to taste
12	corn tortillas, toasted
	Poblano Cream (p. 37)
1	head sliced Romaine lettuce

Garnish

1	small avocado, chopped (optional)

Pick over the crabmeat and discard any bones or cartilage.

Coat a medium skillet with vegetable spray and place over medium heat. Add onion and sauté 1 to 2 minutes. Combine onion, tomatoes, papaya, cilantro, and crab in a bowl. Toss gently to combine without breaking up the papaya or crabmeat. Season with lemon juice, salt, and pepper.

Spread each tortilla with about 2 to 3 tablespoons of Poblano Cream. Top with sliced Romaine lettuce and crabmeat mixture.

Garnish with chopped avocado.

ENCHILADAS

Enchiladas may be rolled, stacked, served in a casserole, or folded, which makes them "soft tacos." In most cases, corn tortillas are traditionally dipped in oil to soften and seal, and unfortunately, to absorb quite a lot of fat. This may be the reason home cooks devised various ways to prepare casseroles with layers of fillings and tortillas, skipping this often messy procedure. Enchiladas are best when rolled and served immediately—another challenge for the 1990's cook who needs to do some advance preparation. Here are some procedures to soften the tortillas and several options for baking and reheating rolled enchiladas.

To Soften/Seal

Skillet Method. To soften and seal corn tortillas prior to rolling, heat a skillet, preferably nonstick, over medium heat. Using tongs to hold the tortillas, spray them one at a time with a butter-flavored spray and then place in the skillet. Turn quickly, 5 or 6 times, until soft and pliable. Remove the skillet from the heat. Fill and roll the tortilla, then return the skillet to medium heat and repeat with remaining tortillas.

Microwave Method. Microwave 2 or 3 tortillas at a time on high for 10 to 15 seconds. Cover the warmed tortillas with a lightly dampened towel while rolling and filling one at a time. This method only softens tortillas. It does not seal them. Flour tortillas do not need sealing. Soften them in a microwave oven or one at a time in a nonstick skillet over medium heat.

To Heat or Bake

To Microwave. Filled enchiladas may be wrapped in plastic wrap, 2 or 3 in a package, and reheated in a microwave oven. This method is good for preparing 3 or 4 servings. The tortillas will not dry out or fall apart (as they tend to do when covered with sauce). Microwave on high to warm, 60 to 90 seconds, and heat the sauce separately.

A microwave oven is particularly suitable for reheating enchiladas because it provides a moist heat and tortillas will not dry out. However, be very careful not to "heat" too long because tortillas can get quite tough.

To Prepare for Baking. Place filled enchiladas, seam side down, in a 9 × 13 Pyrex dish. Brush the tortillas with some of the sauce and cover with plastic wrap. Press the wrap directly on the tortillas. Cover again with foil and refrigerate until ready to use. (If baking immediately, cover with foil only).

Preheat the oven to 400°. Remove the foil and plastic wrap. Discard the plastic wrap. Brush the enchiladas again with the sauce and replace the foil. Turn the oven to 375° and place enchiladas on the middle rack. Bake 15 to 35 minutes; 35 minutes if refrigerated prior to baking.

Heat the sauce separately. If serving buffet style, add the sauce and garnish to the baking dish or lift out individual servings and add sauce and garnish to each serving.

Accompaniments

Traditional accompaniments for enchiladas are rice and beans. Bean recipes include black beans, pinto beans, or a colorful combination of beans. You can also choose one of the rice recipes in this book with compatible flavors and colors. With red sauces, for example, the Mexican Rice and colorful vegetables would be a good choice. Arroz Blanco is a good match for Green Chicken Enchiladas or Spinach Enchiladas. For some of the heartier enchiladas with cheese, you might make a combination plate and serve one enchilada per person along with a chalupa or crispy taco and a Skinny Guacamole salad.

Many of the salsas provide a colorful, light accompaniment. Tomato salsas go with almost anything, as do their variations with black beans, avocado, or corn. Corn or mango salsas go well with tomatillo sauces or red sauces. Tomato-based salsas offer a fresh contrast to cheese sauces.

Garnishes

Fresh, colorful garnishes are suggested for all enchiladas. They provide contrast in texture and create visual appeal. Many traditional Tex-Mex dishes, particularly those with red chili sauces, pinto beans, and Spanish rice create a colorless or monochromatic plate. A small lettuce and tomato salad topped with crisp tortilla strips or a simple combination of corn, jicama, and lime do wonders for enchiladas. For more ideas and information about garnishes, see pages 8–11.

Several fillings and sauces follow. Mix and match them according to personal taste but, do not be limited by these sauces. The Ranchero Sauce on p. 150 goes well with chicken or beef fillings. Tomatillo Sauce for Green Chicken Enchiladas is equally good on Seafood Enchiladas, and the Sour Cream Sauce goes well with chicken, seafood, or wild mushroom fillings. The Cornmeal Crepes on p. 16 are also good with a variety of fillings and sauces. I particularly like these for stacked enchiladas, where fillings are layered between the crepes and served "stacked" instead of rolled.

Mild Tomato Enchilada Sauce

Makes
2 1/2 cups

Use 1 1/2 to 2 cups
for 10 enchiladas
(5 servings)

Fat grams
3.5 per cup
2 per serving

Calories
170 per cup
60 per serving

Making a homemade enchilada sauce is easier than you might think, and the results are far superior to the canned varieties. You can omit the small amount of low-fat sausage, but it gives significant flavor for less than 25 calories and a gram of fat. Either the Smoked Turkey Stock or Fat-Free Stock is excellent for making enchilada sauces, and you will need nothing else to achieve full flavor.

1/2	ounce low-fat smoked sausage, in pieces
2	cloves garlic, minced
1	tablespoon chopped onion
1	tablespoon chopped carrot
4	tablespoons chili powder
1	14 1/2-ounce can beef or chicken broth, fat removed
1 1/2	cups chopped canned tomatoes or tomato sauce
1	tablespoon cornstarch
2	teaspoons vinegar
1/2–3/4	teaspoons salt

Coat a saucepan with a nonstick vegetable spray and place over medium heat. Add sausage, garlic, onion, and carrot, and cook a few minutes. Add about 1/2 cup chicken or beef broth and chili powder and simmer, stirring constantly about a minute. Transfer the sauce to a blender. Add the tomatoes and blend until smooth. Pour the blended sauce and remaining chicken broth back in the same saucepan.

Dissolve the cornstarch in 2 tablespoons water and vinegar, and stir into the sauce. Cook 2 to 3 minutes or until thickened. Cool and season to taste with salt. Thin sauce if necessary with chicken broth or, if you desire a thicker sauce, increase cornstarch to 1 1/2 tablespoons.

Use in any recipe that calls for Tomato Enchilada Sauce.

Advance Preparation: The sauce may be made 1 to 2 days in advance.

SPICY ENCHILADA SAUCE

....

The smooth-skinned red chilies are what give this sauce its assertive flavors. (You will immediately understand how tomato sauce found its way into enchilada sauces.) If you have prepared the Fat-Free or Smoked Turkey Stock, use this in place of the chicken broth. Both stocks give a very rich, meaty flavor to the sauces. The maple syrup and vinegar help balance the slight bitterness from the chili pods. This sauce will please *aficionados* of Mexican-style red sauces. Use it with fried eggs for Huevos Rancheros or with one of the fillings that follows. The sauce keeps well refrigerated for one week, or freeze for another use.

Makes
3–3 1/2 cups
Use 1 1/2 cups for
8 enchiladas
(4 servings)

Fat grams
5 per cup
2 per serving

Calories
208 per cup
75 per serving

3	smooth-skinned, red chili pods or ancho chili pods, toasted, stemmed, and seeded
2	cloves garlic, minced
2	tablespoons chopped onion
1	tablespoon chopped carrot
1	tablespoon safflower oil
2	tablespoons chili powder
1	14 1/2-ounce can Mexican-style tomatoes
1	14 1/2-ounce can chicken broth
2	tablespoons maple syrup
1 1/2	tablespoons red wine vinegar
1/2–3/4	teaspoon salt
2	tablespoons all purpose flour
1/2	cup water
1	8-ounce can tomato sauce (optional)

Preheat the oven to 300°. Rinse the chili pods in warm water to clean and place them directly on the oven rack. Toast for 10 to 12 minutes, then turn the oven off and leave the chilies in the oven for 20 minutes. Cool and coarsely chop into small pieces. Discard seeds and stems.

Sauté the garlic, onion, and carrot in safflower oil in a medium saucepan over medium heat. Cook until softened, then stir in the chili powder and liquid from the canned tomatoes. Add the tomatoes and chili pieces and bring to a boil. Cover, turn the heat off, and let stand about 15 minutes. Transfer to a blender jar and blend smooth.

Return the sauce to the same saucepan and add chicken broth, maple syrup, and vinegar. Dissolve the flour in the water, stirring to remove all lumps, and add to chili mixture. Bring to a simmer, stirring constantly until thickened, about 3 minutes. Taste and adjust salt. If you prefer more tomato taste and less heat, stir in tomato sauce.

If using ancho chili pods, the sauce will be thicker and you will only need 1 tablespoon flour for thickening.

Advance Preparation: The sauce may be made 1 or 2 days in advance.

SOUR CREAM SAUCE

Makes
1 1/2 cups

Fat grams
8 per cup

Calories
180 per cup

There is no sour cream in this sauce, but it has a "sour cream" flavor. Traditional sour cream enchiladas are loaded with both sour cream and melted cheese, adding up to major fat grams and calories. If you use the processed American cheese, the result is more like a cheese sauce.

1	tablespoon light butter
2	shallots, minced
2/3	cup chicken broth
2	tablespoons all purpose flour
1	cup low-fat buttermilk
1	ounce fat-free or light cream cheese
1 1/2	ounces low-fat Monterey Jack cheese or 1 1/2 ounces processed American cheese
	Salt and pepper to taste

Heat the butter and shallots in a small saucepan over medium heat and cook until shallots are softened. Add flour and 3 to 4 tablespoons chicken stock. Stir until the flour mixture is smooth. Add the remaining chicken stock and buttermilk. Stir constantly over medium heat until thickened, about 2 or 3 minutes. Cool a few minutes, then pour into a blender and blend smooth.

Return to the same saucepan and stir in the cream cheese or cheese of choice.

Season to taste with salt and pepper.

BEEF ENCHILADAS

....

	Taco Meat (p. 128)
10	corn tortillas or Cornmeal Crepes (p. 16)
1 1/2–2	cups Mild or Spicy Enchilada Sauce (pp. 140, 141)
4	ounces cheddar cheese, grated
3	ounces low-fat feta cheese, crumbled

Garnishes

Onion rings or sliced scallions
Crispy Greens (p. 8)

Serves
5

Fat grams
23 per serving

Calories
526–541 per serving

Prepare the Taco Meat using either ground turkey or lean ground beef and set aside.

Prepare, fill, and bake enchiladas with method of choice.

Top with both cheese and onions.

Serve two enchiladas per person and garnish with onions and Crispy Greens.

CHICKEN ENCHILADAS

....

Serves
5

Fat grams
11

Calories
390

10	corn tortillas
1 1/2–2	cups Mild or Spicy Enchilada Sauce (pp. 140, 141)
5	cups shredded cooked chicken breast or Seasoned Chicken Filling (p. 13)

Garnishes

	Crema (p. 21)
4	ounces feta cheese, crumbled
2	cups Romaine lettuce, julienne
1	cup fresh diced tomatoes

Prepare, fill, and bake enchiladas with method of choice. Serve two enchiladas per person.

Garnish with a ribbon of Crema, crumbled feta cheese, julienne lettuce, and a few diced tomatoes.

CHEESE
ENCHILADAS

....

2	cups chopped onion
5	ounces low-fat ricotta cheese
4	ounces low-fat cheddar cheese, grated (see note)
4	ounces low-fat Monterey Jack cheese, grated
	Salt and pepper to taste
10	corn tortillas
1 1/2-2	cups Mild or Spicy Enchilada Sauce (pp. 140, 141)

Serves
5

Fat grams
18 per serving

Calories
395−410 per serving

Garnishes

	Onion rings or sliced scallions
4	ounces feta cheese, crumbled or low-fat cheddar cheese, grated
3	radishes, thinly sliced
	Romaine lettuce, thinly sliced

To make the filling, heat a medium skillet over medium heat. Add the onion and sauté, stirring occasionally, until lightly browned, about 4 to 5 minutes. Remove from heat and stir in the ricotta cheese.

Prepare the tortillas with method of choice and fill each one with the ricotta cheese and onion mixture and about 1/2 ounce of each cheese.

Reheat in a microwave oven or bake according to directions. Serve two enchiladas per person.

Garnish with onions, feta cheese, thinly sliced radishes, and lettuce.

Note: You may substitute nonfat processed American cheese for low-fat cheddar cheese.

VEGGIE
ENCHILADAS

....

Serves
5

Fat grams
6

Calories
280

These enchiladas have a cheese, rice, and vegetable filling; however, almost any combination of sautéed vegetables can be used in place of the rice and Ricotta cheese.

1 1/2	cups chopped onion
1	green bell pepper, chopped
1	cup frozen corn, thawed
3	ounces light processed American cheese
1/2	cup low-fat Ricotta cheese
1 1/2	cups cooked white rice
	Salt and pepper to taste
10	corn tortillas or Cornmeal Crepes (p. 16)
1 1/2–2	cups Mild or Spicy Enchilada Sauce (pp. 140, 141)

Garnishes

	Crema (p. 21)
1 1/2	cup spinach, julienne strips
1	cup fresh diced tomatoes

To make the filling, heat a medium skillet over medium heat. Add the onion and bell pepper and sauté, stirring occasionally, until lightly browned, about 5 minutes. Add the corn and American cheese, and stir until the cheese is melted. Add the rice and ricotta cheese and mix well. Season to taste with salt and pepper.

Prepare tortillas with the method of choice and fill each one with a generous 1/2 cup filling. Bake or microwave as directed. Serve two enchiladas per person.

Garnish with a drizzle of the Crema, julienned spinach, and diced tomatoes.

Sour Cream
Enchiladas

....

Sour Cream Sauce (p. 142)

6   scallions, thinly sliced (green and white portion)

5   cups shredded, cooked chicken breast or
       Seasoned Chicken filling (p. 129)

12   corn tortillas or Cornmeal Crepes (p. 16)

6–8   ounces low-fat Monterey Jack cheese (Optional)

Garnishes

2   tablespoons diced fresh jalapeño chilies
       (stemmed and seeded)

1   cup diced tomatoes

1/4   cup thinly sliced black olives

Serves
6

Fat grams
9
(with cheese) 14

Calories
300
(with cheese) 380

Prepare the Sour Cream Sauce. Add the sliced scallions when adding the cream cheese.

Prepare the chicken filling of choice.

Soften the tortillas, 2 or 3 at a time, and fill with the chicken filling. Roll up and place seam side down in a baking dish. Repeat, filling and rolling all the tortillas. Bake or heat with method of choice. Serve two enchiladas per person.

Serve with warm Sour Cream Sauce and garnish with diced tomatoes, fresh jalapeño chilies, and sliced olives. Accompany individual servings with shredded lettuce and thin tortilla strips.

CHICKEN ENCHILADAS WITH TOMATILLO SAUCE

....

Serves
5

Fat grams
17

Calories
400

In San Antonio, these are called "Green Chicken Enchiladas." In some areas, they are called "Enchiladas Suizas." Recipes vary from cook to cook, but in all cases the sauce is practically fat- free.

Tomatillo Sauce

2	cloves garlic, minced
1	cup onion, diced
1	tablespoon safflower oil
10–12	tomatillos, husked, rinsed, and quartered
1/2	cup cilantro sprigs, stems removed
5	parsley sprigs
3	serrano chilies, stemmed, seeded
1/2–1	cup chicken broth — *o lite wine*
1/2–1	teaspoon salt coarse ground black pepper
	Pinch sugar

The Filling

5	chicken breasts, on the bone
2–3	tablespoons chicken broth
1	cup fresh tomatoes, diced
	Salt and pepper
10	corn tortillas
1	cup "Crema" or light sour cream
3	ounces feta cheese, crumbled
8	radishes, thinly sliced

Preheat the oven to 400°. To make the sauce, place a saucepan over medium heat and cook the garlic and onion in the safflower oil until translucent. You may need to add a little chicken broth to prevent browning.

In several batches, put the tomatillos, cilantro, parsley, and serrano chilies in a blender jar and blend smooth.

Add the blended tomatillos and remaining chicken broth to the saucepan and bring to a boil. Season to taste with salt, pepper, and a pinch of sugar.

Season the chicken with salt and pepper and cook with the skin on for about 35 minutes. When cool enough to handle, remove the skin and bones. Shred or cut the chicken into small pieces. Moisten the chicken with the chicken broth, add tomatoes, and season with salt and pepper.

Soften the tortillas in a microwave oven or hot skillet (see p. 137). Roll and seal.

Spoon some of the sauce over the tortillas, then cover and bake at 350° for 15 to 20 minutes or until heated through. Heat the remaining sauce separately. Serve two enchiladas per person, and spoon additional sauce on top. Garnish each serving with a spoonful of the Crema or sour cream, crumbled feta cheese, and thinly sliced radishes.

Advance Preparation: Both the sauce and chicken may be prepared a day ahead.

Spinach Enchiladas Ranchero

Serves
5

Fat grams
14

Calories
360

The Ranchero Sauce is mild but has the distinctive, rich taste of poblano chilies. The sauce is excellent on almost any enchilada, omelette, or egg dish. Try using the Cornmeal Crepes (p. 16) in place of corn tortillas for a light luncheon entrée.

Ranchero Sauce

2	large poblano chilies, roasted, peeled, seeded
2	cloves garlic, minced
1	red onion, chopped
1	tablespoon safflower oil
1	14 1/2-ounce can Mexican-style stewed tomatoes
1	8-ounce can tomato sauce
1	teaspoon red wine vinegar
1/2	teaspoon oregano
1	tablespoon fresh basil
1/2–1	teaspoon salt
1/4	teaspoon cracked black pepper

The Filling

1	cup diced onion
4	tablespoons chicken broth
1/2	cup diced red bell pepper
1/2	cup mushrooms, finely chopped
1/2	cup low-fat ricotta cheese
1	10-ounce package frozen spinach, thawed and drained
1/4	teaspoon cayenne pepper
1/4	teaspoon white pepper
10	corn tortillas

Garnish

3	ounces feta cheese, crumbled

To prepare the sauce, rinse chilies and cut into 1-inch strips. Set aside.

In a saucepan, heat the garlic and onion in safflower oil over medium heat and cook until softened. Add the tomatoes, tomato sauce, vinegar, and reserved chilies. Bring to a simmer and cook, uncovered, 6 to 8 minutes. Add oregano, basil, salt, and pepper.

To make the filling, sear the onion in a saucepan coated with vegetable spray. Add chicken broth, red bell pepper, and mushrooms and cook until softened. Stir in the ricotta cheese, drained spinach, and seasonings. Remove from heat and set aside.

Prepare the tortillas according to directions on p. 137. Roll and seal. Bake according to method of choice.

Serve two enchiladas per person. Spoon Ranchero Sauce on top and garnish with crumbled feta cheese.

Advance Preparation: The sauce may be made a day in advance. The filling is best when made the day you plan to serve the enchiladas.

Variation: Shrimp and Spinach Enchiladas. Fresh chopped shrimp are delicious with the spinach and vegetables. Choose from a Sour Cream Sauce or Qeso and serve with Pico de Gallo.

1	shallot minced
1 /1/2	cups chopped shrimp
1	ounce dry vermouth
	Sour Cream Sauce (p. 142) or
	Queso (p. 38)
	Pico de Gallo (p. 24)

Sauté the shrimp and shallot in a medium skillet using a non-stick vegetable spray. Season with salt and pepper. Deglaze the pan with vermouth and set aside. Stir into the spinach filling.

Prepare the sauce of choice and keep warm. Ladel the sauce over enchiladas, serving 2 per person.

SHELLFISH ENCHILADAS

Almost any combination of shellfish may be used to make enchiladas with equally good results. Lobster and crab are particularly good and make a special dish for entertaining.

Serves
8

Fat grams
7

Calories
221

1	tablespoon light butter
4	jalapeño chilies, stemmed, seeded, diced
3	scallions, sliced (green and white part)
2	shallots, minced
1/4	cup diced red bell pepper
3/4	pound shrimp, peeled, deveined, chopped
3/4	pound lump crabmeat, bones removed or
	3/4 pound each, shrimp and bay scallops
	Salt
1/4	teaspoon cayenne pepper
1/2	cup white wine
1	tablespoon lemon juice
2	tablespoons chicken broth
3	ounces fat-free cream cheese
1	ounce light processed American cheese
2	cups julienne spinach
16	Cornmeal Crepes (p. 16)
	Grilled Tomato Salsa (p. 26)
	or Sour Cream Sauce (p. 142)

Garnish

	Toasted Tortilla strips
2	cooked shrimp, tails on
	Italian parsley

Heat the butter in a large skillet over medium heat. Add chilies, shallots, scallions, red bell pepper, and shellfish. Sauté, tossing constantly, 2 to 3 minutes. Season with salt and cayenne pepper.

Add white wine, lemon juice, and chicken broth and bring to a boil. Remove and strain the cooking juices from the shellfish.

◄ *Shellfish Enchiladas with Grilled Tomato Salsa* (Recipe on page 153)

Set shellfish aside and return juices to the skillet and place over medium heat. Add the cream cheese and American cheese, and stir until cheese is melted and smooth.

Combine the cheese mixture with shellfish and spinach in a mixing bowl. Season with salt and pepper. Soften prepared crepes in a microwave oven. Fill each one with the shellfish mixture, roll up and place seam side down in two 7 × 11 casserole dishes. Cover with foil.

Put the salsa in a saucepan and bring to a boil. Reduce the heat and simmer, stirring occasionally, for 5 minutes. Thin if necessary with a little chicken stock.

Preheat the oven to 400°. Heat the enchiladas, covered with foil, about 20 to 25 minutes. Serve two per person, topped with Grilled Tomato Salsa. Garnish the enchiladas with tortilla strips, whole shrimp, and Italian parsley.

Cheese Enchiladas with Chili

Makes
10 Enchiladas
2 1/2 cups sauce
Serves
5

Fat grams
21

Calories
471

Low-fat cheeses help reduce the fat grams and calories in this Tex-Mex favorite. Significant amounts of fat are also saved by omitting the traditional step of dipping the tortillas in oil prior to rolling. For the best results, use thin corn tortillas.

The Sauce

1/2	pound top round, ground
1/2	cup diced onion
2	cloves garlic, minced
3	tablespoons chili powder
1	14 1/2-ounce can beef broth
1	8-ounce can tomato sauce or
	1 1/2 cups stewed tomatoes, puréed
1	tablespoon all purpose flour
3/4–1	teaspoons salt

The Filling

1	large onion, chopped
6	ounces low-fat longhorn cheddar cheese
6	ounces low-fat Monterey Jack cheese, grated
10	corn tortillas

Garnishes

1	bunch scallions, green and white portion, sliced
4	ounces low-fat feta Cheese, crumbled
2	ounces low-fat cheddar cheese, grated

To make the sauce, place a saucepan over medium heat. Add the beef and sear until well browned. Add the onion, garlic, and chili powder, stirring to break up clumps of meat. Add the beef broth and tomato sauce or tomatoes and simmer 4 to 5 minutes.

To thicken the sauce, stir the flour into 1/4 cup water until smooth and free of lumps. Add a little of the hot sauce to the flour, then add it to the sauce and cook 5 to 6 minutes, stirring constantly. Season with salt.

To prepare the filling, place a skillet over medium heat and spray with a vegetable oil spray. Add onion and cook 2 to 3 minutes until softened and lightly brown. Set aside.

Soften and seal the tortillas as described on page 137. Fill each one with a spoonful of onion and both cheeses. Roll up and place seam side down in a baking dish. Repeat, filling all the tortillas.

Heat or bake the enchiladas according to one of the methods on page 137. Serve two enchiladas per person. Spoon the sauce on top and garnish with cheese and scallions.

Advance preparation: Both sauce and filling may be prepared in advance.

KING RANCH
CHICKEN

....

Every Texan has some variation of this popular casserole dish—a sort of "Enchilada Casserole." It is usually made with a canned soup and enormous amounts of cheese. This version has been lightened by making a lighter sauce and using a low-fat cheese.

Serves
8–10

Fat grams
14

Calories
400

The Sauce

2	shallots, minced
1	clove garlic, minced
1/4	cup dry white wine or vermouth
1	tablespoon carrot, finely diced
1	tablespoon celery, finely diced
1	tablespoon green bell pepper, finely diced
1	14 1/2-ounce can chicken broth
1	cup skim milk
4	tablespoons all purpose flour
1	teaspoon salt
1/4	teaspoon white pepper
2	jalapeño chilies, stemmed, seeded, minced
2	ounces light processed cheese or 2 ounces non-fat cream cheese
1	large onion, diced
1/2	cup each diced red and green bell pepper
1	4 1/2-ounce can diced green chilies
1	10-ounce package corn tortillas, quartered and toasted
8	chicken breasts, boned and skinned, diced
1	teaspoon chili powder
6	ounces low-fat Monterey Jack cheese, grated
1	10-ounce can diced tomatoes and green chilies

Preheat the oven to 350°.

To make the sauce, bring shallots, garlic, white wine, vegetables and chicken broth to a boil in a medium saucepan.

Dissolve the flour in skim milk, then pour slowly into the hot chicken broth, stirring constantly. Reduce the heat to medium-low and cook, stirring, until thickened. Add salt, pepper, minced jalapeño chilies, and processed cheese. Stir until the cheese is melted. Set aside.

Coat a medium saucepan with vegetable spray. Over medium heat, sauté the onion, bell peppers, and chilies until softened. Season with salt and pepper and set aside.

Spray the tortilla quarters with a butter-flavored spray on both sides and place on cookie sheets. Toast in a preheated 350° oven 8 minutes. Tortillas will not be crisp. Put half the tortillas in a 9 × 13 casserole.

Put half the chicken on top of the tortillas and season with salt, pepper, and chili powder. Top with half the chilies and onions. Repeat the layers and pour the reserved sauce over all. Top with grated cheese and undrained diced tomatoes and green chilies.

Bake at 350° for 40 to 45 minutes or until hot.

NANCY'S ENCHILADA CASSEROLE

....

My friend and food *afficionado*, Nancy Dedman, designed a women's club luncheon with this as an entrée. It was served with a light green salad and miniature corn muffins. This version had one-third less calories and fat grams than the original and tested equally well with ground turkey or beef.

Serves
6

Fat grams
14.5

Calories
386

12	corn tortillas

The Sauce

3	tablespoons chopped onion
1/4	cup chopped mushrooms
1/8	teaspoon cayenne pepper
1 1/2	cups chicken broth
1/2	cup skim milk
4	tablespoons all purpose flour
3	ounces fat-free cream cheese
1/4	teaspoon garlic salt
1	4 1/2-ounce can diced green chilies
	Salt to taste

The Meat

2	cloves garlic, minced
1 1/2	cups onion, chopped
1	pound lean ground beef
1	tablespoon chili powder
1/2	10-ounce package frozen spinach, thawed
2/3	cup Mexican-style stewed tomatoes, without juice, chopped
	Salt and pepper to taste
	Egg substitute equivalent to 1 egg
5	ounces low-fat cheddar cheese, grated

◀ *Chicken Margarita with Pico de Gallo, Green Chili Spoon Bread, and Black Bean Sauce* (Recipes on pages 116 and 170)

Cut five tortillas in thirds, then in thin strips, and spray with a butter-flavored spray. Toast in a 350° oven for about 8 to 10 minutes or until crisp. Set aside.

Place a medium skillet, preferably nonstick, over medium heat. One at a time, spray 7 corn tortillas with a butter-flavored spray. Using tongs, heat them on both sides in the skillet, turning often until softened. Place into 10-inch pie pan overlapping tortillas.

To make the sauce, generously coat a saucepan with a vegetable spray and cook the onions and mushrooms over medium heat, stirring constantly. Add the cayenne pepper, stir briefly, then add the chicken broth and bring to a boil. Dissolve the flour in skim milk and stir to remove all lumps. Add a little of the hot broth to the flour and stir in, then add the flour mixture to the broth and cook, stirring constantly, about 3 to 4 minutes. Add cream cheese, garlic salt, green chilies, and salt to taste. Stir to combine and set aside.

To cook the meat, heat the skillet again over medium heat. Add the beef and break up with fork, but allow it to sear until browned. Add onion and garlic and mix in well. Stir in the chili powder, spinach, and tomatoes. Season to taste with salt and pepper. Remove from heat and stir in egg substitute and 2 ounces of the cheese. Put the beef on top of the prepared tortillas. Sprinkle with half the toasted tortillas, then the reserved sauce. Top with remaining grated cheese. Bake in a 325° oven for 30 minutes.

Garnish with remaining crisp tortillas on top.

MIGAS

This South Texas dish probably evolved from a thrifty cook's use of leftover tortillas. I've omitted the traditional cheese and sausage and used an egg substitute to lower fat and calories. This is a fun breakfast to serve to out-of-town guests or for a brunch with friends.

Serves
4

Fat grams
6

Calories
280

3	corn tortillas, cut in thin strips
1	tablespoon light butter
1	cup onion, diced
1	4 1/2-ounce can diced green chilies or
	1 poblano chili, roasted, peeled, and diced
1/4	cup diced green bell pepper
1/2	cup diced tomato
	Egg substitute equivalent to 10 eggs
1/2	teaspoon salt
1/4	teaspoon white pepper
4	corn tortillas, steamed
	Tomato Salsa (p. 26) or Pico de Gallo (p. 24)
	Mashed Beans (p. 19)

Preheat the oven to 350°.

Place the tortilla strips on a cookie sheet and spray with a butter-flavored spray. "Toast" for 8 minutes or until crisp.

In a large skillet, heat the butter over medium heat. Add the onion and sauté a few minutes to soften. Add chilies, bell pepper, tomato, eggs, salt, and pepper. Cook to "soft scramble" the eggs. Before they begin to set, add the tortilla strips and mix in.

Serve the eggs with beans, salsa, and soft, warm tortillas.

Turkey Tamale Pie

Serves
8

Fat grams
11

Calories
368

This is a great way to use leftover turkey. This recipe is also good made with chicken, lean pork, or wild game.

20–24	dried or green corn husks
3	cups shredded turkey (white or dark meat)
	Salt and pepper
1	4 1/2-ounce can diced green chilies or
	2 poblano chilies, roasted, peeled, and diced
1	red bell pepper, roasted, peeled, and diced
1/2	cup masa harina
1/2	cup yellow cornmeal
1	cup boiling chicken broth
1/2	cup non-fat sour cream
1	16-ounce can creamed corn
1	cup fresh corn kernels
1 1/2	teaspoons baking powder
1	teaspoon salt
1	tablespoon sugar
1	cup Mild Enchilada Sauce (p. 140)
1 1/2	tablespoons Parmesan cheese

Thoroughly wash corn husks and soak in hot water for 1 1/2 hours. Shake excess water from the husks. Spray a 10-inch pie pan with a vegetable spray and line the pan with the husks, narrow ends overlapping the pan. Weight down while preparing the batter.

Season the turkey with salt and pepper and toss with the chilies and roasted peppers. Set aside.

Put the masa and cornmeal in a saucepan and place over medium heat. Add the hot chicken broth and stir constantly to avoid lumps. Add sour cream, creamed corn, and corn kernels and remove from heat. Combine the baking powder, salt, and sugar and mix in well.

To assemble the dish, pour half the dough on top of the husks. Top with turkey mixture and enchilada sauce. Add the remaining dough and sprinkle with Parmesan cheese.

Preheat the oven to 350°.

Fringe the ends of the husks to make a decorative edge. Bake on the middle rack for about 1 hour 20 minutes, or until the top is set. Cover the pie with foil if the top becomes too brown.

Cool 5 minutes and cut into wedges. Serve with light sour cream and your favorite salsa.

TURKEY AZTECA

Here is another delicious way to enjoy turkey—especially the dark meat.

Serves
4

Fat grams
5.5

Calories
395

12	mushrooms, sliced
1/2	cup diced red onion
1/4	cup each, diced red and green bell pepper
1/2	cup diced zucchini
12	Cornmeal Crepes (p. 16)
1 1/2	cups Mild Tomato Enchilada Sauce, heated (p. 140)
2	cups cooked diced turkey
2	ounces low-fat Monterey Jack cheese, grated
	Fresh minced cilantro

Coat a skillet with a nonstick spray and saute the vegetables 2–3 minutes. Season with salt and a pinch of cayenne pepper.

Using 3 crepes per person, assemble as follows. Top one crepe with the cooked vegetables. Add a second crepe and top with turkey and enough sauce to moisten thoroughly. Top with the third crepe, cover, and bake at 350° or microwave on high until warm. Serve topped with remaining sauce and garnish with grated cheese and fresh cilantro.

ACCOMPANIMENTS

*. . . vegetables are a beautiful part of a meal when they
are fresh, tender, and used in exciting new ways.*

Albert Stockli

Traditional Tex-Mex plates always include refried beans and
rice, both healthy foods that are just as easy (and just as
delicious) when prepared with less fat and enhanced with
vegetables. The rice dishes in this section are seasoned with
garlic, onions, and fresh vegetables or chilies and are a colorful
complement to enchilada plates or grilled meats and fish.

Vegetables take on a new personality when grilled over
charcoal and are so flavorful you'll not want to use butter. Beans
don't have to be limited to refried pinto beans. Black beans or a
combination of beans, corn, and vegetables make a light
accompaniment that tastes hearty.

In this section you'll find several cornbread recipes that vary
from mini muffins and jalapeño cornbread to a moist, creamy
spoon bread made with fresh corn and green chilies. These
dishes will enhance both the taste and presentation of all your
Mexican favorites, and your friends will be delighted to find
some light alternatives.

◀ *Grilled Salmon with Grilled Vegetables* (Recipes on pages 115 and 173)

MEXICAN RICE

Serves
8

Fat grams
3

Calories
195

Using an assortment of vegetables with rice adds flavor but no fat. This is a colorful and delicious accompaniment to enchiladas or chicken and fish entrées. Substitute whatever vegetables are fresh and seasonal, giving an eye to color and visual appeal.

1	tablespoon safflower oil
1	clove garlic, minced
1	cup chopped onion
1 1/3	cups long grain rice
1	14 1/2-ounce can chicken broth
1	cup water
1/2	teaspoon salt
1	cup diced carrots
1/2	cup each, diced red and green bell pepper
1	cup diced zucchini
1	cup corn kernels, cooked
1	cup frozen green peas, thawed
	Salt and pepper to taste
1	tablespoon minced parsley or cilantro

Heat the safflower oil in a 2-quart saucepan over medium heat. Add garlic and onion and sauté 1 to 2 minutes, tossing constantly. Add rice and continue to cook a few minutes to coat the rice with oil.

Add the chicken broth, water, salt, carrots, bell pepper, and zucchini. Cover and reduce the heat to low. Simmer for 20 minutes, undisturbed.

Remove the cover and add the corn and peas. If all the liquid has been absorbed, add about 1/4 cup additional hot water. Cover and cook 2 to 3 more minutes. Remove from the heat and let stand, covered, until ready to serve.

Stir in salt and pepper to taste and minced parsley or cilantro.

SPANISH RICE WITH GREEN CHILIES

This rice is typical of the rice served in most Mexican restaurants. I've added green chilies to give it a slightly spicy flavor. Mushrooms are optional, but a nice addition.

Serves
8

Fat grams
4.5

Calories
196

2	tablespoons safflower oil
1	onion, chopped
1	medium-sized carrot, diced
3	cloves garlic, minced
1	cup chopped white mushrooms
1	14 1/2-ounce can chicken broth
1 1/2	cups long grain white rice, uncooked
1	cup Mexican-style stewed tomatoes, tomatoes chopped
1	large poblano chili, roasted, peeled, and diced or 1 4 1/2-ounce can diced green chilies, drained
1/2	teaspoon salt
1/4	teaspoon coarse ground black pepper

In a medium skillet over medium heat, cook the onion, carrot, garlic, and mushrooms in 1 tablespoon of the oil for a few minutes. Add about 1/2 cup of the chicken broth, bring to a boil, then remove and set aside.

Heat the remaining safflower oil in a saucepan over medium heat. Add the rice, stirring constantly until all kernels are coated. Add the rest of the chicken broth, tomatoes, green chilies, reserved vegetables, salt, and pepper and bring to a boil. Reduce the heat to low, cover and cook, undisturbed, about 20 minutes or until all the liquid is absorbed and the rice is tender. Stir gently and serve immediately.

Arroz Blanco

*Serves
6–8*

*About
5 cups*

*Fat grams
1*

*Calories
187*

This simple white rice goes well with enchiladas, seafood, or chicken entrées. It takes only a small amount of butter to give a buttery flavor to the rice.

1	cup chicken broth
1	tablespoon light butter
1	cup water
1	teaspoon salt
1	cup long grain white rice
1	cup chopped onion
1	cup corn kernels, fresh or frozen (thawed)
	Salt and pepper to taste

Garnish:

2	tablespoons sliced scallions (green part)
1	tablespoon minced parsley

Combine chicken broth, butter, water, and salt in a 2-quart saucepan and bring to a boil. Add the rice, lower the heat to medium-low and simmer, covered, for 15 minutes.

Coat a medium skillet with a vegetable spray and place over medium heat. Add the onion and sauté, stirring constantly, until softened. You may need to use additional spray to prevent burning. Add onion and corn to the rice, replace the cover, and cook without stirring for 5 minutes.

Stir to combine rice and vegetables and adjust salt and pepper.

Garnish each serving with sliced scallions and minced parsley.

VEGETABLE RELLENOS

....

This is an attractive dish for entertaining that goes well with grilled beef or chicken entrées. Use a variety of yellow, green, or red bell peppers. Poblano chilies may also be used, but will need to be roasted and peeled prior to stuffing (see p. 7). They are spicier.

Serves
6

Fat grams
5

Calories
196

6	assorted bell peppers (red, yellow, green)
2	small zucchini, diced
1	cup chopped onion
2	cups fresh corn kernels
	Chicken broth
1	cup fresh diced tomato
	Salt and pepper
	Fresh cilantro or basil
3	corn tortillas in thin strips, toasted
6	tablespoons picante sauce
2	ounces low-fat Monterey Jack cheese, grated

Slice the tops from the peppers. Discard the stems, dice the flesh around the top, and reserve. Remove seeds and veins. Place the peppers in a baking dish that has been coated with a vegetable spray.

Coat a large skillet with vegetable spray, and place over medium heat. Add zucchini, reserved diced peppers, and onion and sauté, tossing frequently, until lightly browned. Add corn and enough chicken broth to prevent the vegetables from burning. Cook a few minutes or until the vegetables are just tender. Remove from heat, add tomatoes, and season with salt, pepper, and fresh herbs.

Fill bell peppers with the vegetable mixture and top with toasted tortillas, picante sauce, and grated cheese.

Bake the stuffed peppers at 400° 12 to 15 minutes, just long enough to heat the vegetables and melt the cheese.

Note: If using poblano chilies, add 1/4 cup each diced red and green bell peppers to the vegetable mixture.

Corn and Green Chili Spoon Bread

Serves
8

Fat grams
1

Calories
123

This is one of my favorite recipes for entertaining. It holds well in a warm oven up to 30 minutes and is a wonderful accompaniment to grilled fish or poultry or to serve on a buffet table with beans. Individual servings spooned into a fringed tamale husk make an attractive presentation.

1 1/2	cups fresh or frozen corn kernels
1	cup chicken broth
1	cup skim milk
1/2	cup yellow cornmeal
1/2	cup diced onion
1/2	cup diced red bell pepper
1/2	cup diced green chilies
1–2	jalapeño chilies, stemmed, seeded, and diced
	Egg substitute equivalent to 2 eggs
1/4	teaspoon salt (to taste)
1/8	teaspoon white pepper
1	teaspoon sugar
2	egg whites
1–2	tablespoons Romano cheese, grated

Preheat the oven to 350°.

If using fresh corn, cut the corn kernels from the cobs and set aside. If using frozen, thaw before using.

Bring the chicken broth and milk to a boil in a saucepan. Reduce the heat to low. Slowly add the cornmeal, stirring constantly, and cook until thickened, about 2 minutes. Add the corn and set aside.

Spray a medium skillet with a nonstick vegetable coating spray and place over medium heat. Add onion, bell peppers, and both chilies, and cook until softened, about 2 to 3 minutes. Add onion mixture and egg substitute to the cornmeal mixture. Season with salt and pepper to taste.

In a separate bowl, beat the egg whites with sugar until stiff. Fold some of the whites into the cornmeal to lighten the mixture. Fold lightened cornmeal mixture into the whites.

Spray a 2-quart oblong pan with a nonstick spray and pour the batter into the pan. Sprinkle Parmesan cheese on top. Place the pan in a larger pan, partially filled with warm water. Bake for 45 minutes to 1 hour.

You may turn the oven down to the lowest setting, leave the door ajar, and "hold" the spoon bread up to 30 minutes. Allow the oven to cool down by leaving the door wide open for 5 minutes.

JALAPEÑO CORNBREAD

Cornbread is always best when served right after baking because it tends to dry out.

1/2	cup diced onion
1–2	jalapeño chilies, stemmed, seeded, diced
2/3	cup all purpose flour
1	cup yellow cornmeal
1 1/2	tablespoons sugar
1 1/2	teaspoons salt
4	teaspoons baking powder
2	egg whites
	Egg substitute equivalent to 2 eggs
1	cup skim milk
4	tablespoons light mayonnaise

12 wedges

Fat grams 3

Calories 129

Preheat the oven to 400°.

Coat a small skillet with vegetable spray and sauté the onion over medium heat until softened, about 3 to 4 minutes. Add jalapeño chili and set aside.

Combine the dry ingredients in a mixing bowl.

Whip together the egg whites, egg substitute, skim milk, and mayonnaise. Add to the dry ingredients and mix well.

Coat a 9-inch round pan with butter-flavored spray. Pour the batter in the pan and spray the top lightly. Bake for 30 minutes or until puffed and cornbread pulls away from the edges of the pan. Reduce the heat to 350° and bake another 10 minutes. Serve immediately.

CORNMEAL MUFFINS

*Makes
32 miniature
muffins or 12 large
muffins*

*Fat grams
1
(miniature muffin)*

*Calories
34
(miniature muffin)*

These moist muffins are delicious with salads, soups, or entrées. They reheat quite well, but are best when served the same day you prepare them.

2/3	cups cornmeal
1/2	cup all purpose flour
2	teaspoons baking powder
1	teaspoon salt
1	tablespoon sugar
3	tablespoons light mayonnaise
	Egg substitute equivalent to 2 eggs
1/2	cup skim milk
1/2	cup cream-style corn

Preheat oven to 375°.

Combine the dry ingredients in a bowl and stir to distribute the baking powder.

Stir the mayonnaise, egg substitute, skim milk, and corn into the dry ingredients and mix well. Spray muffin tins generously with a butter-flavored spray. Fill cups 7/8 full and bake 12 to 14 minutes for miniature muffins, about 18 minutes for large muffins.

Cool in the pan 5 minutes, then remove using a sharp knife. When cool, store the muffins in sealed bags. Reheat in a 400° oven or microwave when ready to serve.

GRILLED VEGETABLES

Grilling vegetables is probably the easiest thing you'll ever do. The secret is to "keep it simple." Select the freshest vegetables possible, season them well with salt and pepper, and grill over a hot fire.

Serves
4

Fat grams
6

Calories
131

2	large carrots, sliced diagonally
	Light olive oil
	Salt and pepper
2	medium zucchini, sliced diagonally
3	yellow squash, sliced diagonally
1	red onion, sliced 1/2 inch thick
1	red bell pepper, cut in strips 1-inch wide
1	green bell pepper, cut in strips 1-inch wide

Blanch carrot slices in boiling, salted water for 2 to 3 minutes or until tender but still crisp.

Preheat an outdoor grill to make a hot fire.

Brush vegetables generously with olive oil on both sides and season with salt and pepper. Grill on one side until marked. (You may need to drizzle a little oil on the fire to create a flame). Turn the vegetables, brush again with olive oil, and grill on the opposite side. Vegetables should have good markings and be tender when pierced with a fork.

Place grilled vegetables on a baking sheet and keep warm in a 300° oven until ready to serve. Check seasoning and add more salt and pepper if necessary.

Advance Preparation: Vegetables may be grilled in advance. In this case, grill them until just barely tender. Reheat the vegetables under the broiling element of your oven, 8 inches from the element for 1 to 2 minutes. For best results, preheat the pan, and place vegetables on a hot pan.

GRILLED
SCALLIONS

....

Serves
4–6

Fat grams
trace

Calories
123

This is probably the easiest recipe in the entire book and one sure to please onion *aficionados*. If you are able to buy the giant scallions (often available in South Texas), they are the best. We eat these with our fingers, but some people may prefer a knife and fork. Grilled scallions are a good garnish for almost any grilled entrée such as fajitas, chicken, or shrimp.

4	**bunches large scallions**
	Juice from 1 lime
	Coarse salt

Garnish:

	Diced tomatoes
	Lime wedges

Preheat an outdoor grill to the highest setting.

Trim the whiskers from the scallions, clean well, and cut away bruised or brown ends. Leave about 3 inches of the green portion.

Spray the scallions with a vegetable oil and sprinkle with coarse ground salt. Grill on both sides 1 to 2 minutes or until marked by the grill. Squeeze fresh lime juice over the scallions and serve with additional lime wedges.

Mound the scallions on the center of a plate and garnish with fresh diced tomatoes on top. Serve lime wedges with each serving.

CONFETTI BEANS

....

This combination of beans is not only good for you, but it makes a satisfying accompaniment to a simple grilled fish such as salmon, swordfish, snapper, or tuna. Use any combination of beans or peas.

*Serves
6–8*

*Fat grams
1*

*Calories
204*

1	tablespoon light butter
2	garlic cloves, minced
1	cup red onion, diced
1/2	cup green bell pepper
1/2	cup diced red bell pepper
2	tablespoons diced pickled jalapeño chilies
1/4–1/2	cup chicken broth
1	cup black beans, drained
1	cup field or black-eyed peas, drained
1	cup northern beans, drained
	Pinch of thyme
1	tablespoon fresh cilantro
1	cup diced tomatoes, peeled
	Salt and pepper to taste

Heat the butter in a large saucepan over medium heat. Add the garlic, red onion, bell pepper, and chilies and sauté until softened.

Add chicken broth and the liquid drained from the peas or northern beans. Bring to a boil and reduce to thicken the liquids.

Add the thyme, cilantro, and tomatoes. Season with salt and pepper.

DESSERTS

All's well that ends well.
William Shakespeare

The Mexican people, like Americans, have quite a sweet tooth, and "sweets" are quite popular—so popular they are often eaten throughout the day. Candies such as pralines are often likely to follow a meal. Perhaps this is because sugar has a neutralizing effect on lip-searing chilies.

While the desserts in this section are not all low in sugar, they are quite low in fat or calories. Cocoa is used in place of chocolate, skim milk in place of cream, and egg whites replace whole eggs. Fresh fruits, Spanish-influenced flan and custards, or rice pudding are desserts that *can* fit into a low-fat lifestyle quite easily. In this section, you'll also find chocolate, caramel, and raspberry sauces that are very low in fat and add delicious, colorful appeal when drizzled over crepes, a crisp cookie taco, or fresh berries.

◀ *Apple Bread Pudding* (Recipe on page 182)

Caramel Flan

Serves
4

Fat grams
trace

Calories
244

This flan is much lighter than those made with condensed milk, in taste as well as calories. The cornstarch creates a slightly dense texture and is necessary when using skim milk.

1	tablespoon water
1/2	cup granulated sugar
2	cups skim milk
2	teaspoons freshly grated orange peel (no rind)
1	tablespoon cornstarch
	Egg substitute equivalent to 4 eggs
1/4	cup granulated sugar
1	teaspoon vanilla extract

Garnish

	Sections from 1 orange, all membrane removed
8	strawberries, hulled and sliced

Put 4- to 12-ounce custard cups in a 13 × 9 Pyrex dish and fill it one third full of water.

Heat a medium skillet over medium heat. Add water and 1/2 cup sugar and keep on the heat until the sugar turns amber and begins to caramelize. Shake the pan to distribute the sugar. It should melt and be amber in color but not burned. Immediately pour melted sugar in the custard cups, tilting them to coat the bottom.

Dissolve the cornstarch in 1/2 cup of the milk, then add it to the remaining milk and orange rind in a small saucepan, and bring to a simmer over medium-high heat. Stir constantly once the milk is warm.

In a separate bowl, whisk together the egg substitute, 1/4 cup sugar, and vanilla. Slowly add the milk and mix well. Divide between the custard cups.

Bake for 40 to 45 minutes or until a knife inserted in the custard confirms it is set. Remove the cups from the water bath and cool 15 minutes. Refrigerate 3 hours. Run a knife around the edge to unmold flan.

Serve garnished with orange sections and sliced strawberries.

Caramel
Meringue
Almendrado

This recipe is adapted from "Natillas," the New Mexican dessert made with egg whites and gelatin served on a soft custard. The caramelized sugar is easy to do (no fat!) and makes a dramatic dessert.

Serves
6

Fat grams
trace

Calories
337

The Custard

2	cups skim milk
1	envelope custard powder or
	2 1/2 tablespoons arrowroot
	Egg substitute equivalent to 4 eggs
1/4	cup granulated sugar
1	tablespoon amaretto liqueur
2	teaspoons vanilla

The Meringue

5	large egg whites, at room temperature
1/2	cups granulated sugar
1/4	teaspoon cream of tartar
1	teaspoon vanilla extract

Caramel Sugar

1	cup granulated sugar
2	tablespoons water

Garnish

Fresh seasonal berries

To make the custard, heat 1 1/2 cups milk in a 1-quart saucepan over medium heat. Whisk together the custard powder or the arrowroot, egg substitute, sugar, and remaining milk until smooth. Slowly add to the milk, stirring constantly. Reduce the heat to medium-low. Cook 3 to 5 minutes, lifting the pan from the heat if the mixture threatens to curdle. Stir until the custard is thickened and smooth. Add amaretto and vanilla. Strain and cool.

To make the meringue, preheat the oven to 325°. In a clean bowl, beat the egg whites with cream of tartar until they hold soft peaks. Gradually add the sugar, continuing to beat. Beat until the egg whites hold stiff, glossy peaks, then fold in vanilla.

Spray 6 custard cups or 10-ounce souffle dishes with a non-stick vegetable coating spray. Sprinkle lightly with sugar. Place the cups in a large pan partially filled with warm water. Spoon meringue into prepared dishes and bake for about 10 minutes. (Meringues will fall as they cool.) Run a knife around the edges of the cups and invert meringues on serving plates. Pour the chilled custard around each meringue. Refrigerate. (This should be done no more than 2 hours before serving time.)

To finish the dessert, put the water and sugar for the caramel in a medium skillet over medium-high heat. Heat until the sugar melts and begins to turn amber. Once all the sugar is melted and light brown, stir briefly and remove from heat. Let the sugar cool slightly but not long enough to harden (this takes seconds). Pour the caramelized sugar in a thin stream, back and forth in both directions, to drizzle caramel over the meringues. The sugar will harden almost immediately.

Garnish with fresh berries.

COOKIE TACOS

These crisp little shells may be made into sweet tacos or chalupas, the latter being a little easier to make. Fill them with non-fat ice cream and fresh berries and caramel or chocolate sauce, or try the following combination.

The Shells

1/2	cup slivered almonds (1 ounce)
1/2	cup sugar
2–3	tablespoons water (more or less)
1	tablespoon corn syrup
1/2	cup mixed fresh blueberries and raspberries or strawberries (per shell)
2	tablespoons low-fat nondairy topping (per shell)

Raspberry Sauce

1	package frozen raspberries
1–2	tablespoons sugar

Garnish

2	tablespoons Caramel Sauce (p. 188)
	Fresh mint sprig
2–4	fresh berries

*Makes
12*

Serve 1 per person

*Fat grams
4.5*

*Calories
102*

Preheat the oven to 375°.

To make the shells, put the nuts and sugar in a food processor fitted with the metal blade and process until finely chopped. Add water and corn syrup and process again. The batter should be moistened but not "soupy." Let it rest for 15 minutes.

Line cookie sheets with parchment paper. Drop round spoonfuls of batter on parchment sheets. (A miniature ice cream scoop makes uniform "balls" that spread evenly.) Bake 10 to 12 minutes or until balls spread and are lightly browned.

To make taco shells, quickly cut around each cookie and drape over a broomstick handle to make a shell. Hold the cookie in place a few seconds until it begins to harden. If making flat "chalupa" shells, simply cool the rounds on parchment. Store tacos in airtight containers. Remove parchment when ready to use.

Bring frozen raspberries to a boil. Add sugar and boil about 2 minutes. Blend in a blender or a food processor fitted with the metal blade. Strain to remove seeds.

To assemble the dessert, place shells on a serving plate. If taco shells will not "stand," place a few berries on either side to hold in place. Carefully fill each shell with assorted berries and a dollop of topping. Spoon the raspberry sauce on the plate and drizzle caramel over the taco. (To make "chalupas," place berries and whipped topping between two rounds.)

Garnish with a mint sprig.

APPLE BREAD PUDDING

Serves
8

Fat grams
3

Calories
288

Mexican bread pudding was traditionally made with cheese in place of milk. This version uses neither milk or cheese. It is best when served warm, fresh from the oven.

1/3	cup raisins (about 3 ounces)
1	ounce apple brandy
1	cup brown sugar, packed
3/4	cup water
1/2	teaspoon cinnamon
2	large apples, peeled cored and cut in pieces
5	slices low-fat or French bread, crusts removed
	Egg substitute equivalent to 4 eggs
1	teaspoon vanilla
3	tablespoons melted light butter
1	tablespoon cinnamon sugar

Preheat the oven to 350°.

Soak the raisins in apple brandy for 15 minutes.

Bring water and sugar to a boil in medium saucepan. Add cinnamon and apples and simmer 5 minutes. Remove from heat and cool to "warm."

Cut the bread into small cubes and place in a bowl. Add egg substitute, vanilla, raisins, and cooled apple mixture. Toss to coat the bread.

Coat a deep dish 9- or 10-inch pie pan with melted butter. Add the apple mixture and drizzle remaining butter on top. Sprinkle with cinnamon sugar.

Bake 10 minutes at 350°. Turn the oven down to 325° and bake 35 to 40 minutes or until set.

Cut into wedges and serve warm with a low-fat nondairy topping.

RICE PUDDING

It takes a little time to make a creamy rice pudding, whether you use milk, cream, or skim milk. The longer you cook it, the creamier (and better) it gets. If you use arborio Italian rice, the result is even creamier. Raisins or currants are a good alternative when fresh berries are not available.

Serves
4

Fat grams
6

Calories
227

1	tablespoon light butter
1 1/2	cups water
1/3	cup long grain white rice
1	cup skim milk
4–5	tablespoons sugar
1	ounce light cream cheese
1/2	teaspoon vanilla extract
1 1/2	cup fresh raspberries or strawberries
1/4	cup Caramel Sauce (p. 188)

Bring the butter and water to a boil in a small saucepan. Add the rice and reduce the heat to low. Cover and simmer on the lowest setting for 35 minutes or until most of the liquid is absorbed.

Add the milk and sugar and cook, covered, on low heat for 30 to 40 minutes. All of the liquid should not be absorbed. Stir in the cream cheese and vanilla and remove from heat.

Serve chilled with fresh berries. Drizzle each serving with warm caramel.

CARAMEL CREPES

Makes
8 crepes
2 per person

Fat grams
12 each

Calories
269 each

This is probably one of my favorite Mexican desserts. It is usually made with rich Mexican caramel called *cajeta*; however, this lightened version drew raves from my tasters. The crepes are equally good unfilled, topped with berries and caramel.

The Crepes (makes 16)

3/4	cup all purpose flour
1/2	teaspoon salt
1	teaspoon baking powder
2	tablespoons powdered sugar
	Egg substitute equivalent to 2 eggs
2/3	cups water
1/3	cup milk
1	teaspoon vanilla
	Pinch of cinnamon

The Filling

2	ounces fat-free cream cheese
3/4	cup low-fat ricotta cheese
1/4	cup powdered sugar
1–2	teaspoon vanilla extract
3/4	cups Caramel Sauce (p. 188)
2	cups fresh raspberries or sliced strawberries
2	tablespoons chopped, roasted pecans

Put all the ingredients for the crepes in a blender jar and blend on high speed until smooth. Scrape the sides of the blender jar several times. Let the batter rest for 3 to 4 hours refrigerated or at room temperature 1 1/2 hours before using.

Heat a 5-inch skillet, preferably nonstick, over medium heat. Grease the skillet with an oil-dampened cloth. Add a small amount of batter and tilt the pan so the batter covers the entire pan. Cook over medium heat until lightly browned, then turn the crepe and cook the opposite side. Repeat, until all the batter has been used. Stack crepes between wax paper.

Using a blender or food processor fitted with the metal blade, process the filling ingredients until smooth and creamy.

To assemble the dessert, fill each warm crepe with about 2 tablespoons of the cheese mixture and a few fresh berries. Roll up and place seam side down. Repeat, filling all the crepes.

Warm the caramel in a small saucepan or microwave oven and drizzle over the crepes. Sprinkle with pecans and garnish with a fresh mint sprig or a few berries.

CINNAMON CHOCOLATE COOKIES

These light, airy cookies will satisfy your sweet tooth after a Mexican meal. Cinnamon and chocolate are traditional combinations, and these are particularly good with coffee.

Makes 40

Fat grams 1

Calories 34

6	egg whites, at room temperature
	Pinch of cream of tartar
1	cup granulated sugar
1/8	teaspoon cinnamon
2	tablespoons cocoa powder
1/3	cup finely chopped pecans, toasted
1/2	teaspoon vanilla

Preheat the oven to 275°.

Whip the egg whites until frothy. Add the cream of tartar and whip on medium speed until they turn white. Slowly add the sugar, whipping constantly, until the whites are stiff and glossy. Sift the cocoa powder and cinnamon over the whites and gently fold cocoa, cinnamon, and vanilla into the egg whites.

Drop about 1 1/2 tablespoons batter on parchment-lined cookie sheets, several inches apart.

Bake for 35 minutes. Turn the oven off and leave the cookies in the oven for 15 minutes with the door closed.

Cool and store in an airtight container.

Variation: Add 1/2 cup shredded coconut with the cocoa.

Kahlua Pumpkin Cake

Pumpkin is a favorite ingredient for Mexican desserts, particularly empanadas. I tried many ways to "de-fat" this sweet snack, but phyllo dough became too soggy to make a satisfactory pastry, and without fat most pastry is very tough. The Italian dessert *tiramisu* inspired this variation that marries pumpkin, Kahlua, and chocolate in a light, low-fat dessert.

Serves
12

Fat grams
12

Calories
353

Kahlua Sauce

1	cup water
3/4	cup sugar
3	tablespoons honey
1/3	cup Kahlua

1–1/2	cups low-fat ricotta cheese
4	ounces fat-free cream cheese
3/4	cup canned pumpkin
1/4	teaspoon cinnamon
1/8	teaspoon allspice
1/2	cup powdered sugar
4	egg whites
1/8	teaspoon cream of tartar
1/3	cup sugar
1/2	teaspoon vanilla extract
2	packages fresh ladyfingers, without cream filling
	Cocoa powder

Garnish

2	tablespoons Chocolate Sauce (p. 189)
	Chocolate curls
	Mint sprig or fresh strawberry

To make the sauce, bring water, sugar, and honey to a boil in a 2-quart saucepan. Boil for 5 minutes, add Kahlua and continue to boil 3 to 5 more minutes or until thickened. Set aside.

◄ *Kahlua Pumpkin Cake with Chocolate Sauce* (Recipe on page 187)

To make the filling, put the ricotta cheese, cream cheese, pumpkin, cinnamon, allspice, and powdered sugar in a heavy duty mixer or food processor fitted with the metal blade and whip until light and creamy.

In a separate grease-free bowl, beat the egg whites with cream of tartar until foamy and soft peaks start to form. Gradually add the sugar and continue beating to stiff, glossy peaks. Fold the egg whites and vanilla into the cheese mixture.

To assemble the dessert, split the ladyfingers and place cut side up in an 8 × 11 pan. Drizzle with the syrup to moisten all the ladyfingers. Spread half the pumpkin mixture on top. Put the cocoa in a sieve and shake to lightly dust the cheese with cocoa. Repeat procedure, ending with cocoa powder on top. Refrigerate at least 8 hours.

To serve the dessert, pool the plate with the chocolate sauce. Cut into squares and garnish the top with chocolate curls.

CARAMEL SAUCE

Makes
3/4 cups

Fat grams
.5 per tablespoon

Calories
62 per tablespoon

Mexican caramel, called *cajeta*, is made from sugar and rich milk or cream, which is very high in fat and calories. While this version has quite a lot of sugar, the fat grams are minimal. Almost anything tastes better drizzled with a little caramel, and this goes a long way to satisfy a sweet tooth.

1	cup granulated sugar
1/2–3/4	cups boiling water
1 1/2	tablespoons light butter
1/2	teaspoon vanilla extract

Heat the sugar over high heat in a small saucepan. When it begins to brown, shake the pan to distribute sugar. Do not stir until sugar becomes liquid and caramelizes.

Stir the sugar until nearly all lumps are gone and you have an amber liquid. Remove from heat and gradually add the water.

The mixture will sizzle and foam and clumps of sugar will form, but these will melt eventually. Return the saucepan to low heat and cook, stirring constantly, until nearly all lumps melt and the water has incorporated.

Whisk in the butter and vanilla, cook a few minutes, then remove from the heat and cool. Stir occasionally during the cooling process.

Store at room temperature.

Note: If a few sugar lumps do not dissolve, pour the warm sauce through a sieve and discard the lumps.

CHOCOLATE SAUCE

Cocoa powder gives this sauce a very chocolately taste. "Lite" maple syrup gives a silky texture. It's hard to believe there is practically no butter in the sauce. Use this on low-fat ice cream or yogurt or as a garnish for the fruit desserts in this section.

1/2	cup sugar
1/2	cup water
1/3	cup cocoa powder
1/3	cup light maple syrup
1	teaspoon vanilla extract
1	tablespoon light butter

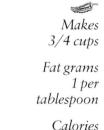

*Makes
3/4 cups*

*Fat grams
1 per
tablespoon*

*Calories
63 per tablespoon*

Combine sugar, water, and cocoa in a small saucepan and bring to a boil over medium-high heat. Stir frequently to avoid lumps. Reduce the heat and simmer for about 2 minutes.

Add maple syrup, vanilla, and butter and cook, stirring constantly, for about 2 minutes. Cool and store in a covered container.

BUNEULO COOKIE SUNDAES

Makes
1

Fat grams
5

Calories
300

For Each Sundae

1	flour tortilla cup (p. 3)
1/2	cup non-fat ice cream or yogurt
1	tablespoons Caramel Sauce (p. 188)
1	tablespoons Chocolate Sauce (p. 189)
3–4	fresh berries (blueberries, raspberries, or blackberries)

Prepare tortilla cups as directed. Fill each one with ice cream or yogurt and drizzle with both sauces.

Garnish with fresh berries.

MEXICAN CHOCOLATE CAKE

Makes
8 wedges

Fat grams
2

Calories
200

This light, chocolaty cake is made without flour or nuts and can be garnished or served in a variety of ways. Pool the plate with Raspberry Sauce (p. 181) and then drizzle the cake with sweetened yogurt or a nonfat dairy topping or arrange fresh berries atop the cake and drizzle with Chocolate Sauce. It is also delicious served warm, sprinkled with powdered sugar.

1/2	cup powdered cocoa
1/2	cup boiling water
4	tablespoons instant or quick-cooking oatmeal
1	tablespoon "light" butter
1/4	teaspoon cinnamon
1	cup sugar, divided use
2	egg yolks
1	tablespoon chocolate liqueuer
2	teaspoons vanilla
5	egg whites
	Pinch cream of tartar

Preheat the oven to 350°

Put the cocoa in a mixing bowl. Add the hot water, oatmeal, and butter. Stir until smooth and then let stand 5 minutes. Add cinnamon, 2/3 cup sugar, egg yolks, liqueuer, and vanilla and mix well.

In a separate clean bowl, beat the egg whites with cream of tartar until stiffened. Slowly add the remaining 1/3 cup sugar in a slow, steady stream, beating constantly, until you have stiff, glossy peaks.

Fold egg white and chocolate mixture together. Coat an 8-inch round Pyrex dish or spring form pan with a nonstick coating spray and transfer the blended chocolate mixture. Bake for 40–45 minutes or until puffed and firm. Cut the cake in 8 wedges and remove carefully with a spatula—it is too fragile to unmold.

Cookie Taco with Raspberry Sauce and Caramel Sauce (Recipe on page 181)

INDEX